Trained by
Sir Nigel Gresley

by
Eric Bannister

edited by Joan Heyes
from conversations with the author

Dalesman Books
1984

The Dalesman Publishing Company Ltd.,
Clapham, via Lancaster, LA2 8EB

First published 1984
© Eric Bannister, 1984

ISBN: 0 85206 809 3

To
Florence Elizabeth Mason

Phototypeset, printed and bound by Galava Printing Co. Ltd., Nelson, Lancashire

Contents

Cover photographs:
Top: Pencil portrait of Sir Nigel Gresley from "The Engineer".
(G.J. Hughes collection)

Bottom: A4 No 4498 'Sir Nigel Gresley' passes Baron Wood on the up Cumbrian Mountain Express, October 1984. **(Gavin Morrison)**

Acknowledgements

We should like to thank the following people for their kind help and advice: Richard Cameron, who started it all; Michael Harris for his valuable suggestions; Dr John Coiley, Keeper of the National Railway Museum at York, for permission to use the Library and reproduce a selection of photographs; C.P. Atkins, J. Edgington, Michael Blakemore and Michael Rutherford of the NRM Library for their care and attentions in supplying the photographs; Mike Esau for picture research; and Mrs Godfrey, P.N. Townend and the G.J. Hughes collection for the loan of photographs.

FOREWORD

I HAVE been asked to write a foreword to this book and I can say at once that, for reasons that you will discover, fewer tasks could give me more pleasure. The story behind the book began in an unusual way.

In October 1978, the A4 Locomotive Society was running a railtour shortly after we had transferred our locomotive No 4498 *Sir Nigel Gresley* from her lengthy enforced stay at Lambton Engine Works at Philadelphia to Carnforth. The programme was to run our train from Leeds to Carlisle and the following morning work a North Eastern Locomotive Preservation Group train from Carlisle to Leeds over the Settle-Carlisle line. It was an exciting weekend as No 4498 had last been over the line in 1967.

We had particularly planned this weekend to include a number of special guests including old friends of the locomotive and the society, amongst whom was Sir Nigel Gresley's daughter, Mrs Geoffrey Godfrey and her family. Unlike most of our excursions, the weather was really miserable. After taking water at Long Preston, we proceeded to Dent, where the clouds were down and it was foggy. It was decided to cut short the stop as we were due to take water at Garsdale only ten minutes farther on.

The guard had given us the right of way and I was about to climb on to the footplate, when somebody told me that there was a man in a wheelchair who used to know Sir Nigel. All I had time to do was to tell him to get into his car and meet us at Garsdale! Shortly after arriving there, I saw the wheelchair and was introduced to Eric Bannister. Mrs Godfrey and her sons also went on to the platform to meet him.

The result of this encounter led to further meetings, for I discovered that he lived in Settle, which is not that far from Carnforth. From then on, Eric and I have corresponded and I have called to see him when I have been able to.

It was about the middle of 1982 that I heard from a friend of mine who is in the publishing business, that he had received a manuscript of reminiscences from Eric Bannister and that they appeared to be good material, though requiring expansion. This is the point at which this book really began to come to life. Joan Heyes, who has been helping the A4 Locomotive Society by selling souvenirs on trains hauled by No 4498, is a writer. She agreed to come with me to meet Eric and to consider the possibility of helping him to complete the book.

As you will discover, Eric had the misfortune to become a victim of multiple sclerosis and by 1982 his ability to type had become impaired. So I had the temerity to ask Joan if she would travel by bus from her isolated home to Settle with her tape recorder and transpose their conversations on to paper. After many hours of travelling and many more at her typewriter, this is the story of Eric's fascinating life as Mr Gresley's 'young man'.

Great credit is due to Eric for his courage; his disability has impaired his speech and it has been a very considerable effort for him to remember so many events and to relate them, especially since he lost all his personal mementoes in a fire. It is particularly happy that some of the photographs in this book were actually taken by Eric and we are so very grateful to Dr John Coiley, Keeper of the National Railway Museum, York, and his staff for permission and help in selecting them.

Eric has magnanimously stated that he is happy for any proceeds from this book to go towards the upkeep of what Mrs Godfrey calls 'my father's beautiful blue engine'. The A4 Locomotive Society Limited is deeply grateful for this wonderful gesture, especially as the locomotive has just undergone a major overhaul at a very heavy price. By buying a copy, you, dear reader, have helped and we thank you most sincerely.

Julian Riddick,
Chairman, A4 Locomotive Society Ltd.

PROLOGUE

I AM now aged 73 and, as I am one of the few persons alive who knew and worked personally for the great Sir Nigel, I have been asked by a number of people what he was like as a man. His admirers will be familiar with photographs of Sir Nigel but, apart from the outline details of his career, little has been recorded about his personality. Unfortunately, I only knew him personally for four years, but I am proud to be able to put my memoirs on record.

Mr Gresley never used my name when speaking to me—he always called me 'My young man'. In the first place, I should like to record that I never heard him speak sharply to anybody. His voice was always modulated, but gave the impression that he was a gentleman with knowledge and authority. He was never snobbish nor did he speak in a voice that ever made me, as his 'young man', feel the slightest inferiority. At the same time, you were always aware that he was the Chief. All those who worked with him personally retained their respect for him as a great steam locomotive engineer.

I was born at Horsforth, Leeds, and my grandfather was the manager of Kirkstall Forge. As a child, I often went to the Forge where the foremen kept their eyes on me and, at a very early age, indeed when I was less than two years old, the red-hot metal of the rolling mills became a familiar sight. Then my parents moved to Doncaster, where I attended the Grammar School. Although of only average academic ability, I enjoyed woodwork and became the school's swimming champion. As there were no educational grants available in the 1920s, my father could not afford to support me in my chosen career as a surgeon. So he paid the £50 premium for an apprenticeship at the nearest engineering works. This was the London & North Eastern Railway's Locomotive Works at Doncaster.

At the slightly late age of 16 years, I applied for an apprenticeship and was accepted by Mr Wintour on behalf of Mr Gresley, whose office was at King's Cross Station. On being shown round The Plant, I was impressed by the sheer size of the place and its enormous machines. It promised to be an exciting place in which to work. So my long railway career began at Doncaster. I little realised at the time how varied my work would be, nor the great excitement that lay in store in the decade to come!

1.

Apprenticeship on the LNER

Doncaster Works

The Mechanical Apprenticeship was for a minimum of five years and was designed to provide a thorough overall grounding in locomotive engineering. There were four grades of trainee: pupils, premiums, premium apprentices and ordinary apprentices. I was a premium apprentice. Pupils and premiums had the advantage of secondary education, but, in theory, all trainees could rise to supervisory positions. The pupils paid £150 to Mr Gresley, who was allowed six pupils a year. They came from all over the world and received no payment from the LNER. They were not obliged to do physical work, although some of them chose to.

I was given a copper box bearing my pay number, 1101, which I took care to inspect promptly on pay day, since it would contain my wages! My early days were full of new skills to learn and fresh acquaintances to make. There were the 'characters' to be looked out for in the Works. There was one clerk, called Frampton, who was straight out of a novel by Dickens. When I went for an order, he would slide back a hatch and his head would appear complete with a twitching walrus moustache. That hatch was always banged shut the minute that business had been concluded! Such encounters made a welcome break from the hard work of the Top Turnery, where I began my training.

The Top Turnery

The foreman of the Top Turnery was 'Trudger' Treece, whose duties included running after the lads and metaphorically (and literally) kicking them up the backside if they did not pay attention to their work. I was taught to use a slotting machine, a shaping machine and a rather large lathe on which I turned piston rings. The younger apprentices were at work on the turret and capstan lathes, engaged on the more repetitive turning jobs. These lathes were within a railed enclosure nicknamed 'The Cage'. Its inmates had to undergo a very messy initiation which involved being spread with lard oil and then feathered! When I asked to be shown 'The Cage', I had

'Trudger' Treece to protect me from the young ragamuffins.

Next, I was assigned to a fitting bench where parts of Stephenson and Walschaerts valve motions were attended to. This was followed by short periods in the tool room where we were taught to grind sharp the various hardened steel machine tools. At the same time, instruction was given on the design of tools and the manufacture of jigs. Finally, I was trained to read mechanical drawings on the marking-off bench.

The Crimpsall

The next stage in Mr Gresley's training scheme for premium apprentices was in the Crimpsall repair shops and I was allocated to No 3 bay. The chargehand was universally known as 'Tagger', and noted for his violent temper. He did not usually have premium apprentices in his section and strongly objected to their presence. I was the first that he had encountered for a number of years and I feel sure that he believed that if I was given all the worst jobs, then I would ask to be drafted!

'Tagger' put me to work on an '01' 2-8-0 goods engine and I was told to assist a fitter in stripping the engine for repair. It was a filthy job and, once the '01' had been stripped, my job was to chip the concrete off the top of the cylinders using a 1¾lb hammer. I was used to a lighter hammer and the frequent slipping of the cold chisel made my hands exceedingly sore and bruised. Having endured this, I was instructed to file up the horns for the axleboxes and then face them up with a scraper. The horns are guides that hold the axleboxes in position on the frames.

I found that the wedges for the horn cheeks needed to be linered and faced in a similar way using a narrow straight-edge from one horn face to the other. All but two passed 'Tagger's' inspection and the few high spots had to be refaced. Next, he told me to erect the valve motion and left me to it. Several weeks elapsed of grinding tedium spent in a pit underneath that 2-8-0 and I struggled with the heavy parts. Fortunately, I became friendly with 'Snowy', who was an excellent fitter, and he helped with the heavy work with the welcome assistance of a hefty apprentice. We managed to wheel the locomotive and replace its boiler and then the '01' was sent out on a trial.

The next engine for repair was a Great Northern Railway 'N2' 0-6-2T which I started to strip on my own. But my work was interrupted by the General Strike of 1926 which resulted in all the premium and pupil apprentices being sent to the running shed at Doncaster Carr to help as best they could.

The General Strike

At Carr Loco, we were at first put to fire-lighting and the general maintenance of its locomotives. Then, rated as volunteer drivers, Foreman Long gave us tickets to carry out repairs if we could. One day, Ahmed Rizk, an Egyptian Government pupil and a great friend of mine, and I were ordered to move three engines as these had to be shunted. Ahmed sat on the point lever as the first two engines passed over. Then, without realising that it would not stay down on its own, he got up. The result was that two of the engines were derailed! Mr Long came up and stood with the two of us, scratched his head and seat and said, 'This is a bugger!' In the event, Bob Vereker, the foreman from the Crimpsall, used the shed's breakdown crane to rerail the two casualties. You didn't need saboteurs with Ahmed around!

At least this interlude allowed me to escape from 'Tagger' and, at the same time, I gained useful experience working on the shed and I got my first taste of working on the footplate. My work also included repairing a faceplate injector and a broken bearing spring among other things. But we had to run the gauntlet of the pickets on the lane leading to Carr Loco. I was twice intercepted and next time I cycled full-speed at them, getting very wet as the lane lay between two dykes! But the pickets erected a barrier so I had to find another way. I had an inspiration. Across the dyke on the right-hand side was Doncaster cemetery and I got my mother to give my an old white sheet which I put over my head with holes enabling me to see. Thus attired, I made my silent way along the road to the shed on my bike. As it was the ghostly light of early morning, the pickets took fright at the moving apparition and scattered. I had to get to work somehow!

Return to the Repair Shops

Once the strike was over, I returned to the 'N2' 0-6-2T back in the Crimpsall repair shops and it was then that I began to see another side to 'Tagger'. He was concerned that the younger apprentices were careless of their safety. Like all youngsters, they couldn't resist kicking things and if they saw something on the passageway linking the bays between the pits, known as the bay crossings, they would kick it. 'Tagger' was right to be vigilant, as accidents were common. One day, a spanner left lying on a footplate was thrown up in the air as the tender went down the centre of the shop. It fell on a man's head and dashed out his brains. Another day, I was out in the yard when a crane was loading cast-iron lamp standards on to a flat wagon. A labourer was standing by the side of the wagon to direct the crane. I'll never forget that man's cries as the lamp standards rolled over on to him and crushed him to death. 'Tagger' said that if they kicked something heavy they could injure themselves badly. So I placed tins of water on No 3 Bay's crossing. My plan worked; the culprits got very wet and stopped kicking things!

One day, Mr Eggleshaw, the Works Manager, came to ask me if I would like to become the (voluntary) secretary of the Pupils and Premiums Association, which was a club with lectures, works visits and social get-togethers. I asked 'Tagger's' advice as he had now become friendly and his response was, 'Take it, the experience will be good for you.' So I accepted the invitation. The post brought me into frequent contact with Mr Eggleshaw and also with Mr Thom, the Mechanical Engineer, and I made many useful contacts through the PPA.

As PPA Secretary it was my task to arrange outings to other railway works and I had a rubber stamp made for the club. On those outings, we used to lark about. I proposed that all new apprentices and pupils should be rubber-stamped on their behinds. The most difficult apprentice to deal with was the late Christian Henry Hewison, author of *From Shedmaster to Railway Inspectorate* (David & Charles). He was a vicar's son and later became a great friend!

We visited Crewe, Derby, Stratford and Gorton as well as the railway-owned docks. With assistance from Messrs Eggleshaw and Thom, we organised a good programme of visiting lecturers. To my surprise, I found that I had a natural aptitude for organisation and the club thrived. Half-seriously, I even asked Mr Thom if Gresley could be invited to speak!

One of the members of the club, an ex-premium himself, would not pay his fees. He was the manager of the Carriage Works and I threatened to pester him daily till he paid up. I was to encounter him again during the War at Dukinfield where he was called 'the Bully'!

But not everything went my way. After I became secretary to the PPA, some premium apprentices went to my workbench and nailed my jacket to the partition between the bays. I had to jump up to retrieve the jacket with the result that the collar was ruined. However, I discovered the culprits and responded by applying lard oil to the armholes of their jackets. No more pranks were played on me after that!

With Snowy's help and advice, we completed the erection of the 'N2' in two weeks. After a few days, 'Tagger' came to me and said, 'You will be transferred because I cannot teach you any more.'

I moved to No 2 machine bay for the next stage of my training. There I worked on the connecting and coupling rods of Pacific locomotives and the work included bedding-on the big-end bearing brasses for all types of rods and the straps and brasses. All went well until I trapped four fingers when fitting the half-moon brass of the centre big-end of an 'A1' Pacific. I was bedding it into the strap of a marine-type big-end. I was forcing the brass down and had my fingers between the brass and the strap. Foreman Grocock sent for the ambulance man as the end of my little finger was completely severed. The other fitters told me to take the end with me to the hospital so I picked it off the floor and expected to hear laughter. There was none. I put my finger end in my pocket, wrapped in a handkerchief. The hospital sewed it on again and sewed up the cuts in the other fingers.

The Shop Manager, Mr 'Little Bob' Vereker, summoned me to work in his office. I was employed on secretarial work and the office clerk taught me to use a typewriter—a skill which was to prove an asset in my career. I bought myself a secondhand typewriter from the Stores Department and thereafter typed my own letters. After several weeks of secretarial duties and technical drawing, I returned to the workshop. 'Little Bob' set me to work on valve-setting and sheave-setting, my last new experience before moving on to the New Erecting Shop.

The New Erecting Shop

I arrived in 1928 when the locomotives being erected were the first 'A3' Pacifics which had evolved from the lower pressure 'A1s', first introduced in 1922. The 'A3s' had the now standard long-travel valves and the boiler pressure increased to 220 psi. I was put to work on an as yet unnamed and unnumbered locomotive, later to become No 2747 *Coronach*. Our job was to straighten the main frames by hammering the frameplate and so stretch the fibres in the steel. Two of us stood facing each other to produce a rhythm of blows and to avoid a mid-air collision of hammers with potentially disastrous results to the strikers: this had to be done accurately. The process was known as 'drawing the plate'. The erection of the 'A3' continued with the positioning of the cylinders and of the frame stays. The fitting of bolts was new to me and the job required great accuracy.

The chargehand was Fred Berry and he gave me much encouragement. He tapped every bolt I had put in explaining the difference in sound between one that was correctly tight and one not fitting evenly over its whole length. In all the time I was with him, he was helpful and explained things as my work proceeded. Each day he came to see me as I was unfamiliar with the three cylinders and conjugated valve gear of the Pacifics, having worked on two-cylinder engines. When I erected the Walschaert valve motion, Fred explained the gear to me stage by stage and left me without any doubts. There could not have been a better chargehand.

When the engine was hauled out of the Erecting Shop, I accompanied him to carry out the final minor adjustments, and Fred left me to attend to something. He went to the back of another Pacific, No 2743, later named *Felstead,* which was being coupled to its tender. Fred climbed up to the cab, holding the cab rail with one hand. Then the shunting engine suddenly jerked. *Felstead* moved backwards and Fred was swung round between the engine and the tender. He was badly injured, but could still speak while being taken to hospital, but sadly, died a couple of hours later. I had been brought face to face with the hazards of my working environment. Fred was sorely missed in the Shop.

Shortly afterwards, when *Coronach* was at the Paint Shop, I asked Mr Eggleshaw if I could go to the Iron Foundry for further experience. He at once agreed and I was there for two months and found the handling of the trowels relatively easy as cabinet-making was my hobby. Once I had got used to the soft sand used in filling the moulds, the men lent me their tools and I even mastered the notoriously tricky swan-neck trowel used for polishing the low part of the mould. It was here that I learnt about the placing of the print nails in the mould. The Smithy was easy after my childhood experience at Kirkstall Forge.

Emboldened by my success, I asked the Works Manager if I could gain experience of the Pattern Shop (usually only the pupils were allowed there), then the Paint Shop, where I learnt the difficult art of painting without leaving brushmarks; the Drop Stamping Shop and the Electrical Shop. The only difficulty was with the Boiler Shop as the boilermakers were suspicious of outsiders; some were friendly but others would not speak to me because I did not have a union card! The result was that I was not allowed to use any tools in the Boiler Shop, although they looked no different from those I was used to. I could see no reason why the boilermakers should prevent mechancial engineers from using tools when, in fact, the fitters needed much more skill and accuracy.

But it was not all work in the Erecting Shop. Apprentices liked to lark about, too. I bought a model dog's turd from a joke manufacturer and it was very realistic. One day, I took it to work and one of the pupils asked if he could borrow it. He put it on Mr

Eggleshaw's office carpet. When the Works Manager arrived, he at once sent for the yard foreman to clear up the mess. But when the foreman inspected closely, it was obviously a model. As secretary of the PPA, I was summoned by Mr Eggleshaw. 'Bannister, what do you know about this? Who's done it?' I replied, 'You don't expect me to tell you that. You know I can't.' He said, 'Tell whoever was responsible not to do it again. You **know** who it was.' We all had a good laugh about it afterwards.

Besides gaining practical experience at the Works, I was enrolled at a specially formulated course for pupils and premium apprentices at Sheffield University's Faculty of Engineering. Mr Gresley and Professor Leigh had prepared the syllabus with a special emphasis on steam and heat engines. The LNER discontinued the Sheffield University tuition after about two years. I took up a correspondence course. Mr Gresley would not sponsor me for the Institute of Mechanical Engineers examination at the time, being of the opinion that I must wait till I had more practical experience. I had not yet met the great man, merely gained a tantalising glimpse of his back from across the yard at the Crimpsall Shops. Rumour had it that he had kicked a bucket of washing water into the pit; in fact he pushed it with his feet.

Shortly afterwards, I again encountered the 'killer' Pacific, No 2743 *Felstead.* I was being trained at the weighbridge where the spring weights were adjusted to those shown on the drawings, or to natural weights, so as to give the correct centre of gravity for the locomotive. The engines were steamed and also tested for leaks which were then corrected. Sometimes, we were lucky enough to go on the trial runs. When *Felstead* was at the weighbridge, the driver fell off the footplate on to the track and broke his neck, being killed instantly. The need to be constantly vigilant was obvious. In fact, *Felstead* was jinxed and in 1960 was involved in a bad accident which nearly led to its withdrawal. After this I was sent to the Carr running shed for training.

Black Carr Running Shed
The District Running Superintendent, Mr Oakes, told me to learn what I could from the Boiler Inspector before reporting to Mr Long for a job. As I was keen to see how things worked from a practical point of view, I climbed the cenotaph-shaped Mitchell coaling plant to see how it was made. It was not easy going up the backward sloping top ladder, but I had no fear of heights as I was used to rock-climbing in the Lake District. When I reached the ground, I was told that Mr Fletcher, the Assistant

13

Running Superintendent, had once ascended the coaling plant, only to be lowered down by rope!

Then I went to see Foreman Long, whom I knew from the General Strike. He set me to work dealing with drivers' tickets and doing any fitting jobs which were reported. I was told to ask him for help if I needed it, but I managed most of the work but was puzzled by an Intensifore lubricator which would not work. As I had not seen one before, I stripped it and found that it was frozen solid with ice. It worked when it was thawed out but I was glad that there were no more about.

The weather remained cold for the Infirmary Rag, which was held annually at this time. We dressed up in all sorts of outfits and terrorised the young ladies of Doncaster with whom we had a poor reputation! However, we had great fun and raised about £500 for the Infirmary. Subsequently, things got out of hand as Hippisley was reported to be walking round town in a mincing manner likely to provoke trouble. Mr Eggleshaw told me to keep people under control, which was a tall order since I had no authority as Secretary of the PPA. As it was, I had great difficulty in keeping the premium apprentices out of the first-class compartments on Works visits!

After that began a most interesting six weeks of footplate experience. My first trip was as third man on a shunting engine around some local sidings. I politely offered the driver my tobacco pouch but he said, "Na na, I'll stick to ma twist.' The next day I was again on a shunting line from Bawtry on the main line and the siding was about half a mile long. The driver let me take over the controls as it was a single line. This time I had some twist in my pouch! This was followed by a trip on the main line to Retford and Grantham on a goods train and a ride to Peterborough on an Atlantic locomotive. All these rides were without incident.

Then I was booked on the 'Ghost Train' at 2 a.m., carrying fish to New England (Peterborough) with a 'K3' 2-6-0 locomotive. My first two trips were uneventful but, on the third night, the exhaust went haywire. So, at New England, the driver said, 'Let's have a look at the front end. Did you see anything from the window?' I had remarked to the fireman at the time that I had seen something. When we looked we saw that the whole of the valve gear had disappeared from the left-hand side! The Running Shed night foreman was called and another 'K3' locomotive had to be substituted.

My next experience was as third man on the expresses to King's Cross hauled by Pacific locomotives. I learned the art of firing the

14

wide fireboxes, including once the famous 'A3' 4-6-2 No 4472 *Flying Scotsman* (which was a 180psi 'A1' at the time). As some of the expresses were night passenger trains, this was an exciting period. It was interesting to learn the signalling system. All the signals were oil-lit semaphores.

One night, when descending Stoke Bank to Peterborough, the train stopped in the station. The driver had asked the fireman to take over and looked deathly pale. When we got out he said, 'I think we hit something.' We ran round to the front of the engine and bent down to examine some hairs on the front rail guard. They were black and brown and we decided that they looked like dogs' hairs. The driver said that it must have been quite large, so we thought that it was probably an Airedale terrier. The fireman told me later that the driver had once hit a man. As we proceeded to King's Cross the driver recovered. The fireman told me that it had been a great shock when the man had been discovered. We wondered how the driver had known that anything had been amiss as neither the fireman nor I had noticed any bump.

My six weeks' footplate experience were over. The Works Manager sent me to the Hydraulic Office where he used me unofficially for technical duties. My first job was to organise a regular examination procedure for the lifting tackle for both the Works and Goods Yard. I had various design and layout jobs to do, including a drawing for 'skids' which were used at Gorton Works. These were made of channel irons and were used for storing boiler tubes for examination and repair. I decided to improve on the design so that, instead of being craned in a bundle to the right height for the repairers to manhandle them, they were rolled one at a time by gravity over a stop to the machines.

At about this time, Mr J.S. Jones, the Assistant Works Manager, asked me to be the secretary of the Boxing Club. I declined the honour because I was busy studying and my work as PPA Secretary took up quite a lot of my time. I took my studies seriously as it was my ambition to have the letters M. Inst. Mech. E. after my name one day. This was more highly prized than a degree in mechanical engineering at Doncaster because it was acquired after the all-important practical training with locomotives as well as the theoretical training. The Boxing Club was where Bruce Woodcock, the National Heavyweight Champion, started his career. I sparred in the ring with him, but unfortunately he did not hit me seriously!

Everybody warned me that by my refusal to take on the secretary-ship, I had ruined my chance for a permanent job at the end of my apprenticeship. Unfortunately, I received a fractured skull in a road accident too and had to spend several weeks in the Infirmary contemplating my future job prospects. In my absence, Mr Gresley visited the Works and saw my new skid design in operation. I was disappointed to miss him but my work had not gone unnoticed.

On my return to work, I was told that a draughtsman had left during my absence. As it had always been my ambition to become a draughtsman, I went at once to see the Chief Draughtsman, Mr Broughton, to see if the job had been taken. He greeted me with, 'Well, if you will go and try to kill yourself, we cannot keep vacancies open in case you recover.'

I was very despondent as times were hard because of the Depression. The number of salaried appointments was severely restricted and many other pupils and apprentices failed to get full-time appointments on the railways. However, after about an hour and a quarter, the phone rang and it was Mr Thom, the Mechanical Engineer at Doncaster, asking to see me. My heart sank as I feared the fate of my contemporaries. He asked me if I had recovered and then told me to report to Mr Broughton.

The best that he could offer me then was a probationary draughtsman's post at a fitter's rate of pay. I was very pleased to be able to go home at lunchtime and tell my mother, who was dying of cancer, that I seemed to have got a job at last. I was particularly grateful as I was the only one of my group of pupils and premiums to remain on the railway. The others were given their cards because of the Depression.

2.   The Drawing Office

I STARTED in the Locomotive Drawing Office after lunch and was at once given a design job to do on a drawing board at the end of the office. From the start, I was never given more senior draughtsmen's drawings to trace, as would usually be the case. This was probably because of my design for the tube skids and other work in the Hydraulic Office which had shown that I had some design and organisational aptitude.

Mr Street, the Assistant Chief Draughtsman, then started to use me for many other jobs. Then Mr Broughton discovered that I understood something of the chemical side of photography and made me the relief photographer in a separate office. The photographer was getting a little old and unsafe because of arthritis so I always went out with him to photograph locomotives and carriages. I liked to have a go at everything.

On Mr Broughton's resignation, Mr Street was promoted to his position. He used me for many interesting design jobs including thermal indicating. This was an exciting time at Doncaster. The detailed design work was being started on the 'A4' Pacifics by Mr E. Windle, mainly on the cylinders. The design of the 250psi boiler was begun by the boiler draughtsman, Mr Hibbeling. Mr Street was working with some ideas of measuring the overthrow of the Gresley 2:1 valve gear on the centre cylinder in response to a letter from King's Cross. Mr Gresley used to do the overall designs and send most of the detailed design work to his team of designers at Doncaster. Thus, at an early stage in my career, I learned the value of teamwork.

Mr Street requested me to assist him with his mail. All his letters were handwritten and my knowledge of typing came in handy. I was given an hour an evening for this duty with the otherwise forbidden overtime payment being allowed, which was very welcome. Then, under Mr Street's directions, we planned the new and larger Drawing Office to be located in the old Top Turnery. The order and estimate had been issued to the Works and it was my job to deal with the progress. As usual, the cost of the work had been under-estimated and I had my first experience of what I called fiddling. It was a question of juggling the overall allocation into different codes for individual tasks. At that time, I could only leave it to the foreman when I told them the Drawing Office allocation.

Mr Street planned the new office and I was given the job of issuing the office supplies after I had taken stock. Mr Broughton had been very mean with these and I was more liberal. When Mr Hibbeling, a senior draughtsman, passed the stores he filled up his pockets till he realised that the allocation was in my hands. He put them all back and it was interesting to note that the use of materials did not increase!

The New Drawing Office

This provided more space than the old office and was called the Central Drawing Office. More men were brought in from Darlington, Stratford and Gorton Works. But the Doncaster people did not like the Darlington people, why I do not know, and turned up their noses at them. TAS said to me, 'Bannister, I want you to try to help me to get people from the Great Eastern (Stratford) integrated in the office.' I said, 'That will be difficult, Mr Street', but eventually, all were integrated.

I was put at a drawing board at the end of the office where I could intercept any chargehands coming into the office with queries about drawings. All people from the Locomotive Works came up some stairs and along a long corridor which passed both main offices. Mr Gresley used to pass my board on his way to see the chief draughtsmen, but never spoke to me as he was on the other side of the half-glass screen to the corridor.

Although the dimensions shown on the drawings had been checked previously by a senior draughtsman who had been doing the job for many years, my task was to see that the part could be erected—and sometimes they could not! As Mr Street explained to me, I was younger and had more recent practical experience.

As I controlled the Plan Printing Room, I had an unusual problem to solve. Mr Green, the printer, found that HNG's initials could not be printed boldly on the drawings because they were written in ordinary as opposed to drawing office ink. He tried to use Indian ink over the back of it, but it is impossible to go over another's signature and Gresley objected. As a result Indian ink was never again used to try to trace his signature. TAS came to me and said, 'Bannister, how can we make Gresley's signature come out so that the people in the Works can see that he has approved it?' I got on to Green who was a good printer but it was a question of adjusting the arc-lamps so that Gresley's initials showed. I suggested that he put a hole in a piece of tracing paper round the signature and increase the light of the carbon arc-lamps on to it. It was an improvement but then we tried thin white drawing paper and that did it. HNG was quite satisfied. All the new detailed drawings were initialled. Any existing drawings of detailed designs that I knew would be suitable for an engine order, I marked with a stencil plate and informed the person to whom TAS gave the job. This worked satisfactorily.

Every query from the Works came to me. Although it was beyond what could be expected of me, I was accepted by everyone in the office. When Eddie Windle was working on the design of the 'A4' boiler, even his cylinder drawings came down to me and, at times, at his request I would tell him what I did not like about it as he was a great friend of mine. Gresley initialled each drawing if he approved it.

There was much visiting between the King's Cross and Doncaster offices in connection with the design of the 'A4'. I met Mr Bert Spencer and got to know him. One day he told me to go at once to the Physical Laboratory at Teddington and take with me a wooden model of the 'A4' to test in the wind tunnel. I was to observe the action of the smoke. I met Professor Dalby whom I had seen before when the streamlining tests had been carried out.

The smoke was simulated by French chalk and took the expected way along the higher part of the boiler and to the cab windows. The fairing at the back of the chimney was shaped level with the top of the boiler and we could think of no way of deflecting the chalk other than by providing some deflectors at the side of the smokebox. Professor Dalby had some stiff card available for trials, so at first we tried the model just as it had been supplied from Doncaster and then lifted it out.

When it was on the table, we noticed a depression in the plasticine fairing behind the chimney, apparently made by one of us when we had lifted out the model from the wind-tunnel. It looked like the mark made by the pressure of a thumb. Professor Dalby said, 'Let's put the wind on and see what happens.' To our surprise, the chalk 'smoke' passed along the boiler, but lifted well above the cab windows. We tried it a second time, with the same result. So Professor Dalby commented, 'It looks as though our accident has found the answer.' We tried again measuring carefully with an instrument now known as a mimic.

Our conclusion was that the slight depression seemingly caused a vortex which caused the French chalk to be lifted clear of the boiler top. This dip in the chimney fairing was at once made in the fairing of all 'A4' engines as instructed by Mr Gresley to both Doncaster and Darlington Workshops.

On the fortnight before it was due out, TAS and Windle came and said, 'What is required for the 'A4', Eric?' I gave him a list of five designs. Two were allocated. TAS left Windle with me. I asked, 'What about the rest?' He replied, 'You'll do them, all three! Work what hours you want but you can do them quicker than anyone else.' I worked three nights till midnight and other nights till nine or ten.

The three drawings were of schemes for oil-box lubrication, sand gear (which had been passed round the office and no one knew how to do it!) and cylinder cocks. I left the sand cocks till last. The cylinder cocks were easy but the oil-box lubrication took longer. I did not draw every pipe but Doncaster used it for the building. The sand-box was awkward. I could not find out how to get round the front corner of the firebox. Then I remembered the catalogue for Bowden X cable and drew a scheme based on my findings. Links were impossible. We were doubtful whether HNG would approve. I stamped them. Gresley looked through them, paused over one, then initialled it. I asked TAS what he said. He commented, 'This is a new design and it is a good thing to have other new details!'

1935 was a very exciting year in my life. Apart from the design work on the 'A4', I accompanied Mr Johnson to Barkston to take the photograph of *Silver Link* in its grey paint. His arthritis made the 15'' x 12'' camera difficult to handle. Later in the year, I printed very large enlargements which were then framed. These were very awkward to print because of the lack of contrast between the grey-painted locomotive against a light sky. The enlarger was originally at Gorton on the GCR and, once again, Johnson could not handle it. The framed prints were sent to King's Cross for Mr Gresley.

Early in 1935, Mr Street took me with him to King's Cross with some tracings for Mr Gresley to sign. Unfortunately, I did not manage to see him. However, I was made a full Grade C Draughtsman so I bought a house in Doncaster with a view to getting married. My marriage coincided with the introduction of the 'Silver Jubilee' train that September. Thus we saw the fruition of all our efforts in this highly successful venture.

Shortly afterwards, TAS told me to accompany him again to

London and on this occasion I was interviewed by Mr Gresley. He offered me a job as his junior technical assistant. He was a quiet man and informed me that he was very busy and that I was to assist Mr Spencer. Then he looked at me and said, 'I shall ask you many questions on many subjects, young man.' Then, he took two draws on his pipe—which I later found to be a typical Gresley mannerism—and laid it at the right-hand side of his desk. I shall never forget his words: 'You must never give me a wrong answer under any circumstances,' then two more draws on his pipe, 'You must always remember I am very much senior to you; yet I am **asking** you.'

I had gone in feeling very nervous, but never again felt any nervousness. Mr Gresley, or HNG as we called him, was a gentleman and I never heard him raise his voice to anybody. At first, he saw me if required. Otherwise, Spencer went in to see him when summoned on the intercom. I went only when Spencer was not at the office and, on such occasions, HNG was always very courteous and stated his requirements.

3. Junior Technical Draughtsman to Mr Gresley

AT LAST I had met the great man and was to be working close to him. As Bert Spencer's assistant, I saw quite a lot of HNG. Bert was very pleasant to work for and first of all sent me out to find lodgings. I was wandering round Islington, suitcase in hand, when a lady in Women's Army uniform approached me and told me to be careful. She found me decent lodgings in Finsbury Square with a double room. This meant that my wife could stay with me while we looked for a house. I was allowed a month's lodging expenses but Bert Spencer got me a fortnight's extension during which I managed to sell my Doncaster house and buy a house at East Barnet.

My first job was to read the monthly technical journals, making a note of any articles that I thought HNG should read. The page number and even the line number was noted on a postcard pinned to the relevant magazine, so that the Chief did not have to waste his time. Of course Bert guided me. Any trade publications were also scrutinised and sent to HNG for his information.

Some of my reminiscences from this period may show why I had such a great regard for HNG as a person. His ability as an engineer is unquestioned, and emphasised by the Gresley engines that have been preserved, but I should like to give the reader an idea of the wonderful character he was, together with the influence he had on the rest of my career. The effect of that first interview remained with me for the rest of my working life. By his patience and willingness to listen to a raw recruit he won my loyalty and respect. He made me want to give him all the help that I could—and that unsparingly.

The junior office in which I worked was very airless with one door opening into the office used by Messrs Spencer and Newsome and the back entrance looking out over Platform 11 of the Suburban station. One day, I was taken sick and I heard later from Dr Henry, my own doctor, that HNG had phoned him and taken him to see the office within a few hours. My illness was caused by the lack of fresh air in the office as we were right up under the roof. The office had not been long in use by Mr Gresley's department. HNG cut through the 'red-tape' and very quickly had an intake fan installed.

As Senior Technical Assistant, Bert Spencer usually dealt with HNG and I usually attended to the requirements of the Assistant CME, Mr O.V. Bulleid, who was also usually very patient. A very clever man, Bulleid was rather eccentric and he had some strange ideas. Indeed, he seemed to have a new one every week and of these, one in a year would be brilliant. I had to develop his ideas and sometimes thought he was treading the thin line between genius and madness! One day he rang through the intercom and asked, 'Bannister, can you tell me if the driving wheels on one side of an engine are larger than those on the other?' I was completely taken aback and could not imagine what was behind the question. I replied, 'No sir, they are all the same size.' He simply commented, 'I see,' and put down the phone. So I went along to his chief clerk who was still there despite the late hour. I found out that it had been a contractor and not a technical man with Bulleid when he asked the strange question. Obviously he knew the answer but his head was whizzing with technicalities and he asked me without thinking or as a joke. He would ask, 'How do they get round curves?'

In 1937, when Bulleid took up his appointment as Chief Mechanical Engineer to the Southern Railway HNG said little about his departure. After that, I had to assist D.R. Edge who took over as Assistant CME. Bulleid was an interesting person in many ways, a very nice man and interested in everything. One day Bulleid asked me to try out a pencil to see if it would wear longer and print up more clearly on the arc-light printing machine. I did a bit of marking on a piece of tracing cloth and found that it was easier to print, tougher and less brittle than other pencils. Mars pencils were ordered at Doncaster and elsewhere after that. Simple things like that were not too much trouble for him. BS used to say, 'What other mad idea has he got?' His ideas, many of which wouldn't really work, are typical of some of the Southern engines that he produced. Some of these were good in many ways but, like him, a bit eccentric!

My early time at King's Cross was taken up largely with office work and in generally assisting Bert Spencer (BS), Bulleid or occasionally, Rupert Hart-Davies. On one occasion Hart-Davies and I were on the platform at 11 a.m. when we should have been in the office. We met HNG who came up and said, 'I suppose you two are going for a coffee. Go and enjoy it but when you return H-D, call to see me. There is no immediate hurry and it will wait until your return.' HNG was always considerate to his staff and knew that we would not abuse his trust.

Mr Gresley used to send for BS whenever he used a scale ruler and we had only boxwood ones with chipped edges. So as I knew the stores procedure from Doncaster, I ordered five new ivory-edged scale rules: one for HNG, one for Bulleid and one each for BS, Newsome and myself. But I had by-passed the Chief Clerk, who was rather annoyed and objected to my order. BS took them to HNG who had merely said, 'I shall use these very often.' The Clerk was told that the Technical Office only ordered tools which were essential—I never again had my orders queried!

After a few months came my first outside job for HNG. He had said to BS, 'I should like to know why water is getting into the leading axleboxes of the tenders of Pacific locomotives.' BS discussed it at length with me and, as neither of us had any ideas as to what was causing the problem, I volunteered to go out and see at first hand. I went to Mr Webster, the King's Cross Shedmaster, but neither he nor the drivers had any ideas as to why the axleboxes were being affected. So I designed a wooden platform to fit in front of the vacuum brake cylinders with a view to watching the scoop pick up water from the troughs.

I knew from footplate experience when I was an apprentice that water came over the back of the tender when it overfilled, but was convinced that the overflow could not get forward to the axlebox. BS mentioned my plan to HNG who agreed, provided that I understood that it was at my own risk. Mr Webster arranged for the erection of a safe platform. The test took place over the troughs at Scrooby as I had been to see my wife's parents at Doncaster.

With Inspector Jenkins on the footplate, I climbed onto my platform well covered with two rubberised mackintoshes to protect me from an inevitable wetting. The more I thought about it, the more I suspected that the water was being thrown forward by the water scoop. From my vantage point under the tender, I hoped to see the action of the water. It was rather hair-raising as I used the brake cylinders as a backrest but I had to be careful as they tip forward towards the cab when the brake is applied!

After passing over the troughs, the first thing I heard was Sam Jenkins' voice, for thanks to a violent blow in the midriff from the water, I was speechless. However, I remembered seeing that the scoop had thrown the water forward and sideways. Obviously, I was very satisfied as I had proved what I had already begun to suspect. Water built up like a wall inside the scoop so that some was pushed out forwards. The problem was solved by the insertion of a vertical plate in the mouth of the scoop to split the water, thus avoiding the build up of pressure inside the scoop. The next day BS was able to give HNG the answer to his 'I should like to know' which was his usual form of inquiry and I had survived my big adventure!

Overtime payment was still not allowed by the Chief Clerk and the Staff Clerk. The latter had HNG's rubber stamp, and exercised almost dictatorial rights over the office staff. Unfortunately, HNG was too preoccupied with his engineering work to be fully aware of the problem. In fact, HNG's only failing was that he had almost no time for administrative matters except when he visited the mechanical engineers at the workshops and gave them verbal instructions. But there was an exception. A third copy of all letters signed by him was circulated for staff to read, so that we would know what was going on. Private staff matters were not included in the third copy procedure.

I had finished reorganising the whole of the drawings catalogues, the British Standards specifications and the photographs to save HNG's time and so he started to send me on outdoor duties more often. I had an unusual assignment to visit Cardington to view a number of steam engine models which had been offered to the LNER and the LMS. Whilst at Cardington, we saw the hangar where the ill-fated R101 airship had been built. The model engines were at a private house and I selected a good working model of the Patrick Stirling No 1 which was true to scale. HNG had it on a table in his office for a while and then it went to the General Manager. The LMS was represented by a certain Mr Stanier, of whom I had not heard at the time!

Then came a visit to Scotland to investigate complaints that 'N2' 0-6-2Ts had derailed on the Edinburgh-Dunbar-East Coast section of the main line. I was surprised to find them very steady despite their wheel arrangement and lack of a leading truck. On the first Sunday, I asked the driver to try to attain 60mph on our run to Dunbar, light engine. We reached 58mph but nearly emptied the boiler of steam. For the return trip, the driver made what was known as a 'jimmy' using two wires weighted by fishplates found at the lineside. The 'jimmy' was placed over the top of the blastpipe, to sharpen the blast and thereby improve the engine's steaming. With a clear run, we could reach a higher speed without pumping the boiler dry. Unfortunately, the signals were against us. I was sworn to secrecy by the driver!

After speaking to BS on the phone, arrangements were made for another 'N2' to be made available, but I could find no difference in the running of the two engines. But no more derailments took place south of Edinburgh, although complaints came of 'N2s' derailing on the Glasgow suburban lines and I was sent to ride on the footplate to investigate. For over three weeks my trips were without incident, and when there were derailments, before I could reach the location, it was too late to find the reason and no marks were to be seen!

After three weeks spent in Scotland a derailment at Parkhead was reported to me. As usual, all had been cleared up before I arrived from only a few miles away. So, feeling like a spy, I sat on a lineside fence (and it was very cold) with my eyes glued to the driving wheels of every engine that passed over the site of the derailment. After about three hours, a train approached at about 20-30mph and, as it passed, I felt sure that I had seen the end of the sleeper dip as the driving wheel had passed over it. So I rang Mr Philips, the Assistant Motive Power Superintendent, to send two platelayers immediately. In fact, he sent three men whom I directed to move the top ballast carefully. They dug down vertically, taking care not to leave any loose ballast near the sleeper end. My 'hunch' had been correct for under the end of the sleeper was a hollow space about six inches deep. The ballast around Glasgow was cinder and not granite and another phone call from the signalbox to Mr Philips revealed that he already knew of the problems of cinder ballast!

I hastened to get my train home to report to BS. HNG asked to see me first thing in the morning. After my verbal report, he rang the Chief Civil Engineer and said, 'Ingols, I knew it was not my engines in Scotland. Obtain a report from your Running Department people in Glasgow.' I heard no more, for he looked at me with his usual slightly twinkling eye which indicated approval and just nodded. I went back to tell BS what HNG's reaction had been.

One day, to my surprise and consternation, a copy of *Shipbuilding* came with the other copies of the technical press. I knew nothing of ships, so I asked BS what I should do about it. BS said that HNG had been appointed to be chairman of a National Committee for Shipbuilding, which he said was a prelude to a higher appointment for the Chief. He advised me to list items of national interest and not call attention to merely technical details. Eventually, all was revealed when his knighthood was announced in the King's Birthday Honours. Despite his new title, Sir Nigel remained the same modest HNG that we had always known and admired so much.

Sir Nigel never failed to make sure that we knew when royalty was expected at King's Cross. We were allowed to watch from the office windows and our wives were allowed to join us for the occasion. We were also invited to attend the unveiling of the nameplates of the 'A4's to be named after the Dominions. We stayed at a discreet distance in case he needed us. Our wives were also welcome if they were interested. I was impressed by HNG's modesty when the 100th Gresley Pacific, 'A4' No 4498, was named after him.

Sir Nigel's interest in the performance of his Pacifics led him to consult with the drivers and firemen on engines standing with trains at the end of Platform 10. Sometimes he sent for 'Bertie' to discuss the drivers' reports and sometimes for Inspector Sam Jenkins. BS usually kept me advised of the subjects of discussion. Nothing was too much trouble when it came to footplate comfort and efficiency.

One day, when BS was away, HNG asked me to ride on the footplate to investigate a driver's report that the Pacifics were inclined to 'nose' at speed. I arranged with Sam Jenkins to ride on 'A1s', an 'A3' and an 'A4' to York, Newcastle and Edinburgh. Finding that the Pacifics did nose at speed, I discussed the matter with BS who instructed me to examine the drawings for a possible cause. As I could not find anything, I suggested that it might be the Cartazzi axlebox used on the trailing truck and he sent me out to ride again until I found the reason!

The Cartazzi axlebox wedge slides were intended to centre the engine again after following a curve but I noticed a jerk as the centring action took place. From the footplate it was unsafe to lean out far enough to watch the behaviour of the axlebox closely, so I arranged with Top Shed to construct a wooden seat suspended from the footplate. Bernard Adkinson, the Assistant Running Superintendent at King's Cross, arranged several runs around the Shed sidings to give me a chance to get used to the very restricted movement when strapped to the seat. The proximity of the coupling-rod crank-pin bearing was rather alarming if I glanced over my shoulder but otherwise I felt quite safe. Light engine runs were arranged for the next day. I did not tell BS of my proposed adventure as he would not have agreed, but Bernard and I were quite satisfied that it would be safe if great care was taken.

The next day I rode on an engine and, with only slight movements of my head, was able to see that the sudden jerks which I had noticed from the footplate were due to the wedge slides sticking and then suddenly centring again. This was not dangerous, but the jerk caused was inclined to cause the fireman's shovel to strike the side of the firehole door when he was firing. Not only that but the movement at the back of the engine might also have an influence on the noseing action at the front end.

BS and I discussed the fact that the Cartazzi slides were designed to have an angle of 1:7'' and he asked me to calculate how the engine weight would be shifted if the angle of the slides was altered.

Calculations showed that an angle of 1:11 would be more suitable. BS spoke to HNG who discussed what I believed I had discovered. HNG was very interested and at once summoned his chief clerk to take a letter. For the first time, HNG asked us both to remain and hear the contents of the letter which instructed all Works to alter all Cartazzi axleboxes to a slide slope of 1:11 as soon as possible. Then he told me that once he had spoken to Mr Street I should continue to ride on the footplates of Pacifics.

When the first Pacific with the altered axlebox entered traffic, I rode on it and noticed an appreciable improvement. However, the jerking may have stopped but the noseing continued! The engine was *Felstead* but I survived the ride! BS told me to await the arrival of the Doncaster proposals before I went out again. When they came, BS and I found that HNG had told Street to alter the laminated springs on both driving and carrying wheels, so I had to await any results before riding again. When I saw that the drawings showed alterations to the number and thickness of the laminated springs, BS told me to continue with my footplate rides but in particular to investigate the springing of the bogie. I found that the thickness of the plates of the carrying wheel springs needed a slight adjustment.

The bogie spring plates were unaltered, but the noseing needed more investigation. Back I went to my drawing board for I had noticed that the Pacifics were sometimes inclined to roll and that this required controlling. I designed a T-shaped bracket with a slot extending between the two frames of the bogie, the slot bearing a vertical and renewable strip of lead about ⅛" thick which would be marked by the proximity of the main frame when the engine rolled. The bolt used to control the bracket was the side control bolt.

BS took the drawing to HNG who approved it and loaned us a 'mimic' for showing the profile of the lead. Bernard Adkinson made the bracket for me at Top Shed and I set out for Edinburgh to test it. At each station, I drew round the lead profile. After examination by HNG, he instructed Doncaster Works to make and fit brass brackets on both the main and bogie frames with a space between them. The faces of the brackets were lubricated to slide together when the engine rolled. When this was bolted in position, I rode on the footplate and found that the alteration prevented undue rolling while the noseing action was considerably reduced and only noticeable at very high speeds. Once again his 'I would like to know' had been answered.

My office companion was Leslie Nicholson who meanwhile was engaged on high-speed braking trials with Norman Newsome, his boss. They were dealing with the Westinghouse Brake Company about the design of a quick-acting brake valve to improve the braking performance of the 'Silver Jubilee', 'Coronation' and 'West Riding' trains. Although it meant giving up Sundays, I was pleased when Norman Newsome borrowed me from BS to accompany Leslie on the trials. Slack adjusters were fitted to both locomotives and carriages, together with the quick-acting brake valves. Norman used us to measure the exact distance at which the Westinghouse equipment had brought the train to a stop.

First, we used an unmodified train so that any improvement could be found on the newly equipped set of coaches. The measurements had to be accurate, so Leslie and I took with us two 60ft tape measures joined together. With these we measured the distance from the left-hand buffer to the nearest pre-arranged signal. The distance between signals was of course known. Leslie and I used to look out for the stop and jump off as quickly as possible. This was done unofficially but, with practice, we could jump off at 15mph. The signal engineer was anxious to clear the line as quickly as possible and nothing was said!

Back at the office, the comparative distances were measured and a report made to HNG who was the instigator of the Westinghouse brake valve fittings. Several of the Westinghouse team came with the train to Peterborough to make their own assessment.

I continued to prepare the drawings from Doncaster and elsewhere for BS to take to HNG. I remember designs for the 'V2' 2-6-2 passing through the office and noticing that many of the details were based on the well-tried designs of previous locomotives. We called the 'V2s' 'miniature Pacifics'. At the same time, the 'B12' 4-6-0s, a Great Eastern Railway design dating from 1911, were being redesigned at Darlington to carry a round-topped boiler. This was to the disgust of BS, who did not approve. In fact, BS told me that when he had objected, the Chief had commented, 'Well, I've got to find something to keep Thompson amused!' That is the only time that I heard of a derogatory remark by Gresley about anybody.

Then there was much excitement over the special run of the old and new 'Flying Scotsman' trains in 1938 in which a typical train of 50 years ago would be compared with HNG's new coaching stock for the 'Flying Scotsman'. Patrick Stirling's 4-2-2 No 1, which had been preserved on withdrawal, was prepared at Doncaster for the occasion. No 1 had been out of use for some time and ran hot when working light engines from Doncaster to King's Cross, although it made it under its own steam. I was awaiting news of its arrival at Top Shed so that I could ring HNG with the latest news. At about 7 p.m., Bernard Adkinson informed me of No 1's misfortune.

He could not get fitters out to repair the engine and asked me if I would go and give him a hand. I left immediately and we began by dropping the 8ft diameter driving wheels on the wheel drops with about an inch to spare! Then we worked together to remetal and refit the axleboxes. Having scraped and fitted them, Bernard said, 'I couldn't tell my men to do this, but I'm going to make sure it doesn't run hot.' He then picked up a round-nosed chisel and scraped the axlebox across the white metal and the brass to make a groove in which the oil would be held almost like a reservoir when the axle turned. After we had replaced the wheels on the drops, I went to Bernard's office and phoned my wife because we knew that neither of us would arrive home much before breakfast. Then I reported the circumstances to Sir Nigel. At about 6.30 a.m., Bernard sent the engine on a trial run and two hours later phoned to say that everything was in order.

We had invitations to ride on the 1888-style train. The Stirling Single pulled the vintage carriages from King's Cross and I rode in the first compartment of the leading coach to Stevenage. The Press then transferred to ride in the new stock pulled by 'A4' No 4498 *Sir Nigel Gresley*. Bernard and I hung back when the train filled up, but Sir Nigel came along and said to us, 'Get on, you two. We've got the signal.' However, we told him that we would prefer to return to King's Cross on the footplate of No 1. To this, HNG replied, 'You'll miss a very good meal, but if you prefer to go on the 8-footer, do. I wish I could come with you!'

Bernard and I enjoyed our run back to King's Cross and No 1 reached nearly 70mph, and its riding was surprisingly smooth. Both of us felt that we could not miss this opportunity having spent much of the night preparing the engine for its special occasion. To our satisfaction, No 1 did not run hot. It was a day that I shall always remember.

My next outside assignment was to investigate complaints of engines priming (carrying over water into the cylinders) in Copenhagen Tunnel. So I rode through the tunnel and discovered that when an engine primed very black hot water splashed over the driver and the fireman. In the first place, I went to see the chemist who said that the water being used at King's Cross was overdosed with softening agent and consequently too soft. London water is hard and had to be treated in order to prevent furring—bad enough in a kettle but disastrous for the boiler of a steam locomotive! So I reported to BS, and, reading the third copy of one of his letters the next day, saw that HNG had given instructions to the chemist and to the water-softening plant to reduce the amount of chemicals used. This ensured that no more priming would occur.

By this time, the test runs for the quick acting brake valves were almost finished and HNG told Norman Newsome, the Senior Carriage Assistant, that he could 'have a go'. In great secrecy, a speed run was arranged in conjunction with one of the Sunday brake tests. As I had assisted at some of the tests at Norman's request, on July 3rd 1938, I was present on the train when the Doncaster 'A4' No 4468 *Mallard* headed out of King's Cross with the 'Coronation' set of coaches and the LNER dynamometer car. For the benefit of the layman, the latter was fitted with instruments to record by stylo on paper rolls : speed, distance, power at the drawbar, etc, of the locomotive.

The Westinghouse people were surprised to see the dynamometer car added to the set of articulated 'Coronation' coaches as this would mean that the day's run would not be comparable with previous tests. However, we proceeded to Barkston, where we turned on the triangle. D.R. Edge, the senior LNER representative, told the Westinghouse team what was proposed and offered them a taxi if they did not wish to return with us. They declined!

At Barkston, Inspector Sam Jenkins asked me to help him to go beneath the engine and douse the middle big-end with superheater oil as a precaution against possible overheating. Mr Robson, who was in charge of the dynamometer car at Darlington, told the Westinghouse team the details of our proposed speed attempt. Then we got the signal to get away and Driver Duddington turned his hat back to front—he was that sort—and off we went!

I sat with Norman Newsome at a table in one of the first-class vehicles. HNG had loaned Newsome a large stopwatch which he used to time the distance from milepost to milepost and so estimate the speed. Approaching Grantham we slowed down as there was a permanent way check at 24mph. Naturally, we were disappointed as we wanted a good run up to the top of Stoke bank. Even so, we passed the summit at 74½mph and our speed gradually increased down the bank. I noticed that my cup of tea had not spilt although the tea was moving about.

Then I said to the group: 'I wonder what's happening at the back end?' So I immediately made my way through to the guard. He was rostered as a spare guard and I asked: 'Everything all right down here? Any particular jerks?' He said: 'Roiding quoite well. Yes, yes. It's roiding awroit, s'awroit.' He was a real cockney! I said: 'You realise that we're travelling at a very high speed?'

He looked out of the window and said: 'Well, Oi'm only a goods guard and Oi don't judge speeds like this.' So I said: 'When I left to come down here the speed was about 115mph.' He just said: 'Well, s'roiding awroit.'

So I returned to the centre of the train where I asked Norman Newsome what speed we were doing and he said: 'Over 120'. Then Bernard Adkinson said: 'I think we'd better go up nearer the front, Eric.' So we went to the first vestibule behind the dynamometer car. He took the left-hand window while I took the right. We leaned out to see if we could smell the stink bomb which was inserted in the hollow crankpin of the middle big end and would be set off if overheating occurred.

We kept calling across to each other when suddenly Bernard called out: 'Can't you smell anything, Eric? Your nose is better than mine.' So I said: 'I haven't smelt anything yet.' Then, 'It's gone. I can smell it!' So Bernard immediately signalled to Inspector Jenkins to steady up. Back at our table, Norman, who had felt the slight touch on the brake, said that the speed then had seemed to be 125mph.

Coasting down through Tallington, we had a conference with Mr Edge and all the railway people to formulate a plan of action for the arrival at King's Cross because we knew that the Press would be waiting. At Peterborough, *Mallard* went to the slip points and on to New England Shed while the station stand-by ex Great Northern Atlantic took over. Mr Edge phoned Sir Nigel at Watton and gave him the news.

On arrival at King's Cross, as the youngest and most agile member of the team, I dropped off the train, ran over the central bridge to my office where I had a number of photographs of the 'A4' and returned to the platform. Meanwhile, Mr Edge had invited the Press into the dynamometer car to look at the record charts. They did not realise that this was done to divert their attention from the Atlantic, which was taken on the slip road to Top Shed while they were occupied. The plan worked.

Mr Robson extracted the charts and BS told me to trace them for HNG the following day. Sir Nigel told the daily newspapers of the record. When tracing the charts, I found that they showed a peak of 126mph but the Chief declined to mention this as the duration was less than a mile.

Bernard Adkinson went to Doncaster, where *Mallard* had returned home under her own steam. He saw the axle and reported to HNG, in the presence of both BS and myself, that in spite of some alarming reports, the damage was no worse than any other

Class '01' 2-8-0 in the Crimpsall Erecting Shop showing the overhead cranes. This was the first class of locomotive on which I started work as an apprentice on the LNER. (**NRM**)

Left: Sir Nigel Gresley. (**Mrs Godfrey**)
Right: Class 'A3' 4-6-2 No 2747 **Coronach** in the Crimpsall where I learnt many skills on this locomotive under the watchful eye of Chargehand Fred Berry. Note the experimental smoke-lifting equipment. (**NRM**)

Coronach after general overhaul specially posed for the Works photographer. (**NRM**)

Class 'A3' 4-6-2 No 2743 **Felstead** which claimed the life of Fred Berry in the Erecting Shop. It became known as a jinxed locomotive as it claimed another life at Doncaster and made me aware of the dangers of my working environment. (**NRM**)

The locomotive frames, smokebox saddle and cylinders of the new class 'A4' Pacific under construction at Doncaster Works in July 1935. (**NRM**)

The first class 'A4' 4-6-2 No 2509 **Silver Link** on the weighbridge at Doncaster Works, September 29th, 1936. (**NRM**)

October 25th 1935.

The Chief General Manager,
KING'S CROSS.

"THE SILVER JUBILEE" TRAIN.

I have just been looking up the dates of the various occurrences incident to the construction of the Silver Jubilee Train.

March 5th, 1935.

High speed run made between King's Cross and Newcastle, after which you suggested the possibility of making a high speed steam train to provide a four-hour service.

March 11th 1935.

The outline diagram of the suggested train was sent to you.

March 26th 1935

Your proposal was approved by the Directors.

Orders were immediately given to Doncaster to prepare the necessary drawings for the engine and the train and to order the necessary materials. A large amount of work was immediately thrown on the Drawing Office.

April 17th 1935.

Cylinder drawings submitted for my approval.

Patterns had then to be made, which took about a month.

June 6th 1935.

Outside cylinders cast at Gorton.

June 7th 1935.

First inside cylinder cast at Doncaster.

June 26th 1935

Engine frames laid down in the Doncaster Erecting Shop.

September 7th 1935

Engine completed and put into steam.

With regard to the carriages, a decision had to come to as to the panelling and the use of Rexine, and full models of sections of the dining car and compartments were constructed at Doncaster. In the meantime the carriage underframes were being made at York and these were received Doncaster on 27th May 1935. The construction of the bodies immediately put in hand and the whole of the train was completed on 17th September 1935.

I think it is very creditable of my department that only twenty-five weeks elapsed from the date the order was and a start was made on the drawings until the train was actually completed.

(sgd) H. N. GRESLEY

Gresley's outline to the Chief General Manager of the LNER of the remarkably fast progress in constructing the 'Silver Jubilee' train; featuring the building of the new class 'A4'. (NRM).

Sir Ralph Wedgwood's reply and Gresley's letter to Doncaster. (NRM)

COPY

THE CHIEF GENERAL MANAGER,
LONDON & NORTH EASTERN RAILWAY,
KING'S CROSS STATION, LONDON, N.1.

RXL.RLW/III(A)   26th October 1935.

PERSONAL

H. N. Gresley, Esq.,
Chief Mechanical Engineer,
King's Cross.

My dear Gresley,

20/23/23/1   "THE SILVER JUBILEE" TRAIN.

I have yours of the 25th and am very much interested to see the chronicle which you have compiled as to the progress of the Jubilee train from its first inception to its completion. I agree with you in thinking that it is a record which does very great credit to your Department, and in particular to Mr. Thom and to his staff at Doncaster. I am glad to see also that Gorton had its share in the work and played its part as well.

One of the most remarkable features of the undertaking has been that the locomotive and train prepared at such express speed have acquitted themselves in commission with such complete success.

I hope you will convey my thanks to Mr. Thom and his assistants as well as to your staff up here, who have, I know, had a very large share in the success achieved.

Yours sincerely,

(sgd) R. L. WEDGWOOD.

H. N. GRESLEY
CHIEF MECHANICAL ENGINEER   Letters to be addressed

TELEPHONE TERMINUS 6300   KN/L   THE CHIEF MECHANICAL ENGINEER
TELEGRAPHIC ADDRESS   LONDON & NORTH EASTERN RAILWAY
"MECHANICAL CO WESTCENTRAL RAIL,   KING'S CROSS STATION
LONDON   LONDON

REFERENCE
20/23/23/1   30th October 19

R. A. Thom, Esq.,
DONCASTER.

"THE SILVER JUBILEE" TRAIN.
Your Ref.G.11400/1.

I send you herewith a copy of a letter which I addressed to the Chief General Manager with regard to the Silver Jubilee train, with a copy of his reply dated October 26th, and shall be glad if you will convey Sir Ralph Wedgwood's thanks to your staff in the Locomotive and Carriage Departments for their share of the work in connection with the Silver Jubilee train.

Encl.

Class 'A4' 4-6-2 No 2512 **Silver Fox** hauling the up 'Silver Jubilee' train near Abbot's Rippon in 1936. (**Soole/NRM**)

Class 'A4' 4-6-2 No 2509 **Silver Link** with the 'Coronation' train in blue livery at King's Cross Station, June 16th, 1938. (**Box 219/NRM**)

Celebrating the jubilee of the railway 'race to Edinburgh' in 1888, Stirling No 1 with a set of period coaches hauled a special train to Stevenage Station where passengers transferred to the modern express hauled by class 'A4' No 4498 **Sir Nigel Gresley** for the rest of their journey to Barkston, Stevenage, June 30th, 1938. (**Hulton Picture Library**)

Class 'A4' 4-6-2 No 4468 **Mallard** shortly after building with the up Yorkshire Pullman near Brookman's Park. On July 3rd, 1938, this locomotive reached 126mph on the descent of Stoke Bank, thus creating a world speed record for steam which has never been broken. (**Ian Allan/George R. Grigs**)

The 100th Gresley Pacific to be built, class 'A4' No 4498 **Sir Nigel Gresley** was named after the designer at Marylebone Station in 1937. Sir Nigel was presented with a model of the locomotive and is pictured with his senior colleagues. On Gresley's immediate right is F. Wintour, who accepted me for a Doncaster apprenticeship, next to him is A.H. Peppercorn (a real gentleman known affectionately as 'Pep') and my immediate boss, Bert Spencer, is holding his hat. On Gresley's left in order are: R.A. Thom, O. Bulleid, whom I assisted before he left to become CME of the Southern Railway, H. Broughton, senior draughtsman at Doncaster during my apprenticeship, F.H. Eggleshaw, the WM whom I knew from my days as secretary to the PPA, Edward Thompson and Tom Street, who succeeded Mr Broughton and introduced me to Gresley. (**P.N. Townend collection**)

Women at work during the war at Gorton Works where I was very happy overseeing engine output and where the men were such good workers. (**NRM**)

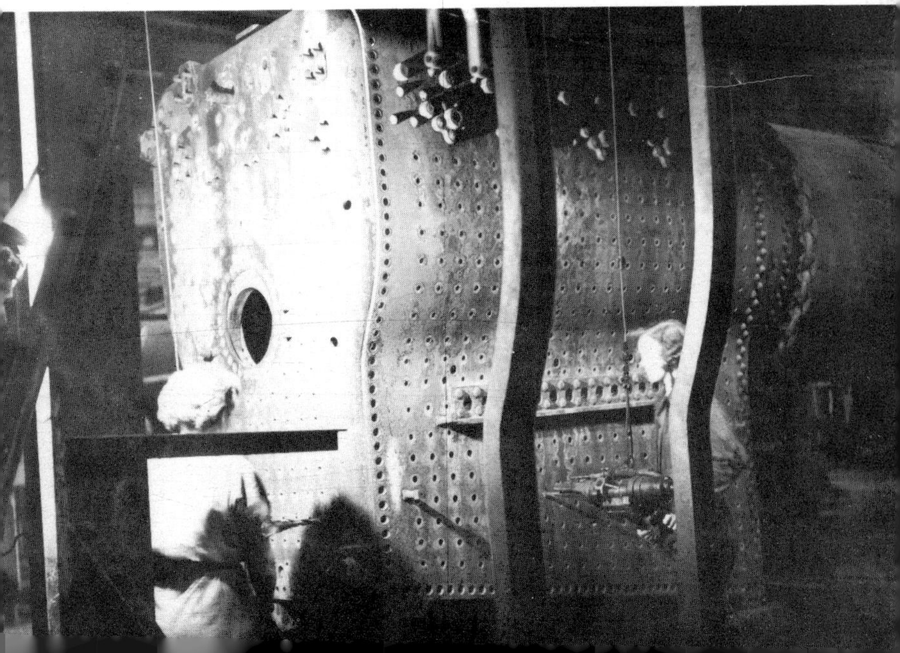

Men working at Gorton during the war in a cage that I designed. (**NRM**)

Bomb damage to a class 'N2' at King's Cross. I had many dealings with this class of locomotive when I was Shedmaster at Hornsey just after the war. (**NRM**)

hot-box. However, HNG decided that, to be on the safe side, the axle should be changed but not scrapped. Bernard Adkinson did not think it was necessary as there was no real damage except to the brasses.

Sir Nigel asked for reports from Norman and me about the riding of the carriages on the record run and was pleasantly surprised to hear that they rode more smoothly than normal. I voiced the opinion that the critical speed seemed to have been passed. He then talked about the possibility of regular and higher speeds. Norman, Bernard and I thought they would be possible but, after HNG had spoken to the Chief Civil Engineer, he told BS that there were places on the East Coast main line where the permanent way still had 40ft rails such as on the lower sections of Stoke Bank, and that these needed relaying before higher regular speeds could be sustained. However, Sir Nigel had seen his great 'A4' Pacific design proved as an enormous success that had captured the public's imagination. Had it not been for that 24mph check at Grantham, we might well have achieved the magic 130mph!

Although the excitement of the record run was a high-spot in my career, I still had many footplate thrills ahead of me. BS was rather fastidious in this respect and certainly the footplate is a dirty place. His reluctance to get covered in smoke and coal-dust was to my benefit.

Shortly before the record run, HNG said ruminatively to BS and me: 'I should like to know why my engines are faster than those of the LMS.' This was a major problem. BS, who was a much better steam locomotive engineer than me and who had been the main advocate of the use of long-travel piston valves on the 'A1s', had no answer to HNG's enquiry. So I went to the drawing board and puzzled over the drawings I knew so well. The indicator diagrams for the 'A1' locomotives I had traced for Tom Street at Doncaster provided no clues although TAS came to my office and discussed them. But BS told me we must find an answer. Suddenly I had a hunch that it must be in the passage of steam.

Unofficially, I bought a number of platform tickets at Euston and also obtained drawings of the cylinders and steam pipes of various LMS locomotives and compared the designs with those of the LNER Pacifics but there were no obvious differences. So, laboriously I made use of all the theory of steam I could think of. I traced the passage of steam from the regulator to the cylinders, but found nothing in the curves which would cause enough friction in the steam pipes to cause an obstruction. I graphed steam expansion, and that mysterious property called entropy, as well as calculating the ordinates for every ten degrees of the revolution of the wheels.

My investigations were somewhat cloak and dagger but led to the discovery that there was a restriction at the blastpipe top. Earlier, a jumper top had been tried on the 'A1' Pacifics at Doncaster while I was in the Drawing Office and of course *Silver Link* had been fitted with one but they had a tendency to become carbonised. BS was doubtful when I presented my findings but my investigations had shown me that our own Pacifics could benefit from modification to the blastpipe.

Two days later, HNG summoned me on my own to his office and briefly glanced through the graphs. Then he said that it would take a long time to examine them and asked me to draw up a chair at the front of his desk. He rang the bell for Mr Love, the messenger, to bring us some coffee and as we drank, he said in his usual quiet way: 'You know, young man, it is a long time since I was at school and I cannot quite follow all your theory, but you have given much thought to this and I believe that you are right. Although it is a long time since I was at school, I can still understand your reasoning.'

Then he asked me to pull up a chair beside him at the desk, commenting: 'It will take a long time to examine all these drawings.' He looked at the graphs one by one and asked a number of questions. After about an hour, he picked up his pipe and took his customary two puffs saying: 'I think you smoke a pipe', at the same time pushing his tobacco pouch across and inviting me to fill up. He went through the graphs once more and said again: 'I know that you have given much thought to this and I believe that you are right. The design of the blastpipe is the restriction on the steam flow and prevents the steam from escaping freely into the chimney and into the atmosphere. This causes a slight back pressure which slows down the rotation of the driving wheels. I must keep an appointment at the Club but will write a letter to Doncaster for them to send me proposals for the exhaust to be less restricted.'

The third copies of his letters were brought to BS first thing the next day, and I noticed the letter asking for a trial with a Kylchap cowl to the chimney. BS told me that HNG, on receiving the drawing, replied with an instruction to Doncaster to cast a blastpipe with two nozzles. HNG then asked BS and me for our views. BS discussed it with me and spoke to HNG. He said that it had been shown that a double blastpipe was necessary because the restriction was at the top of the pipe, and not in the cowl. Thereafter, double blastpipes were fitted to the last four 'A4s', *Mallard* of course being one of them. Mr Edward Thompson still favoured the Kylchap cowl but Tom Street came to King's Cross and saw my graphs. He agreed that the cowls could not influence the passage of steam inside the pipes, but might help the smoke through the boiler tubes.

Thus, as a result of our teamwork, my investigations had led to an improvement in the Gresley Pacifics! Unfortunately, money was short, so the findings were not extended to their logical conclusion of trials on other classes of locomotive. This being 1938, there was much emphasis on speed and the streamlined image of the LNER.

There was still much to be learnt from being close to HNG. The main emphasis of Gresley's management training was always to show by example rather than to preach methods. He was unfailingly courteous and prepared to listen to other points of view. Often he would invite me to his office for consultations and my assessments of investigations and derailments. I had some experience of the latter from my footplate days at Doncaster and after an accident I used to assemble the broken parts for HNG. I learnt much from his brilliance in assessing an accident. When the Senior Inspecting Officer from the Ministry arrived, there were seldom many queries as HNG gave his reasoning aloud. Very often, the recommendations were suggested by HNG himself. He was completely unbiassed and correct. Neither the LNER nor the trade unions escaped his true assessment. Many times in my later career, I had the benefit of his complete impartiality.

After a spell of office work, BS sent me to Aberdeen for more rides on the 'P2' 2-8-2 engines. My experience confirmed my earlier assessment that the long wheelbase was not suitable for the East Coast main line north of Edinburgh. Smooth marks on the tread and tyre flanges showed that I had not been misled and that the curvature on this section of line caused the 'P2s' to jerk as the wheel centred itself.

On the second of my runs with 'P2s' the driver leaned out of the cab with me and said that he had noticed the jerks before but did not know the cause. By special arrangement we had the same 'P2' No 2005 *Thane of Fife* that had taken us from Edinburgh and the same crew. The wind was at gale-force when we crossed the Tay Bridge and the remains of the old piers could be seen plainly despite the state of the weather. I couldn't help imagining what it had been like on the night of the disaster. On this run, the wind was enough for bits of coal to be blown off the fireman's shovel.

I travelled with one foot on the engine footplate and one on the tender footplate in order to gauge any relative movement in their heights. What with pieces of coal flying and swirling coal-dust, my face became rather sore and I had to keep my eyelids half-closed. Crossing the Forth Bridge conditions weren't quite so bad but, even so, I could scarcely see the bridge girders through the rain. The driver and I called out together, 'There it is', when the engine jerked. The variation in the heights of the two footplates was very obvious. The complaints from the Motive Power Superintendent at Dundee were thus borne out and I headed home.

The weather improved for my journey south on the footplate of an 'A3' but the light was rather poor. The tender was full of coal and the large lumps stood out against the sky. Although the fireman was strong, he was tiring by the time we approached Peterborough, so I went through the coal hole in the tender to help him by shovelling coal through to the engine footplate and so make firing easier. I pulled the coal lumps down with the pricker before they could fall on me. We arrived back at Top Shed with only 2 cwt of coal left.

I reported to BS before going home. Although it was late, usually someone would be in the office. Either I or BS or both of us, would wait to see if HNG needed anything before he went home. We waited for Mr Love to tell us that we were not needed. On one occasion I put in for overtime and Harper, the Chief Clerk, objected. BS informed HNG who told Harper, 'There is always someone at the Technical Office every time I come back and do they claim overtime for it? This should be paid.' And it was.

The following morning BS sent me up to see Gresley who was fascinated by my report on the 'P2s' in Scotland. He said, 'What I'd like you to do next, young man, is to see if you can devise a means of mechanical firing for 'P2s' with application to other Pacifics.' I found this a tall order and designed several schemes which did not satisfy me. While I was engaged on this work, two more assistants arrived. One was J.S. Jones, whom I knew from Doncaster, and the other was A.E. English from the Great Eastern. Jones was known as the 'Welsh Cockney' and English was so brilliantly theoretical that Gresley could not make him out.

I said to BS, 'What am I supposed to do with these two coming round? They know more theory than I do!' I had the task of translating their explanations into ordinary English. Jones and English were usually both right but they could not understand each other! BS said, 'Don't worry, Eric, that's what you're here for.' So I became something of an interpreter and this saved Sir Nigel's precious time, allowing him to sum up a subject quickly and then make a decision.

One of English's ideas was that the 'B17' 4-6-0s did not ride well because the centre of gravity of the engine was not the same as that as adjusted by the bearing springs. I consulted my weight books and found a difference of eight inches. English said that this created a couple and so changed the centre of gravity in service. To prove this, I arranged for a 'B17' to be weighed at Stratford Works, then run for a short distance over curves in the Works' sidings, then weighed again. English was right: the spring weights **had** altered. After our adjustments, I had a lengthy ride on a 'B17' on the Great Eastern section and found that the engine rode better and the weight as shown on the diagram did need altering. I reported to BS who agreed to speak to Sir Nigel about it.

The drawings I made for the mechanical firing of locomotives never went for HNG's approval as I was loaned to Rupert Hart-Davies to give him assistance with coaling plants, turntables and mechanical installations. H-D was very busy with his literary endeavours at the time, particularly in writing accounts of the Vitry Testing Plant, which had so interested O.V.Bulleid. With his public school education, H-D was adept at literary expression.

Gresley had a sense of humour which was put to the test one day when he was at Stratford Works. He went to the Running Shed and climbed on the footplate of an engine. The driver challenged him, asking, 'Have you got a footplate pass?' When HNG said, 'No, I haven't', the driver said, 'You're not allowed on an engine without a footplate pass' and sent him down. Gresley went across to the Locomotive Running Superintendent and obtained a pass. He told the driver, 'You were quite right, driver, but I may tell you that I am H.N. Gresley.' With the broadest smile I have ever seen, HNG told me the story himself. He was highly amused by the incident.

HNG was a very pleasant man to work for. He did not like interruptions to his train of thought, so BS and I waited until he asked us—with the well-known twinkle—for our opinions. We presented the facts as we found them, knowing that HNG would make some comment which would automatically cause an assessment or opinion from him and so lead to further conversation. He would always consider carefully before reaching a decision and we were never kept in suspense because of the 'third copy' procedure. When I first went to King's Cross, BS had warned me that HNG did not appreciate criticism of his marine big-end nor of his conjugated valve motion, but that otherwise he encouraged original thought.

That this attitude was genuine was borne out when he asked me,

'What do you think about pulverised fuel?' I replied that I had not thought about it, but that I knew that they had experimented with pulverised fuel on the Great Central. So Sir Nigel said, 'Get Harper to see if there are any papers about the Great Central trials.' Harper said that he didn't think that there were any, which was quite true. I went up to Gorton and there were no records at all, but the Gorton people told me that it had not been a success.

My next assignment was to go to Hatfield to investigate an accident on the main line, in which a 'V2' had been derailed. I was to collect the damaged parts of the engine. There were no curves which could have caused a speeding engine to derail, nor were there any signs of a broken rail although some were badly bent. I carefully examined the brake pull-rods, pins, etc, and marks clearly indicated that a pull-rod was obviously the cause of the derailment. Detailed examination of the forward pin and washer was possible, as the washer was separated from the pin and rod. There were marks on the rail and ballast. The outside of the rod pinhole and washer were smooth.

I used the procedure of analysis used in my presence by Sir Nigel on previous occasions. I assembled all the damaged components with the help of BS at the office for HNG to examine. Mr Edge was to take the place of the Chief in his absence with some minor infection. I thought that BS would accompany him but I was asked to go instead to the Ministry of Transport enquiry to be held by the usual inspecting officer, Colonel Mount.

The time approached and I had not been called to produce the evidence. The Chief Inspecting Officer was due to arrive, so I took the components to Sir Nigel's office. The MOT Inspector arrived with a large retinue of technical assistants but still there was no sign of DRE, so I went into HNG's office on my own. Colonel Mount was not there and the Chief MOT Inspector introduced himself as Colonel Trench. He addressed me as the accepted railway officer and, as Sir Nigel was wont to do, I gave my assessment and proposed my remedy. This was that a groove should be cut across the thick washer, with a round depression for the head of the split pin. It would then be impossible for the pin to become loose. Colonel Trench liked the proposal.

Sir Nigel returned about a couple of days later and immediately sent me to report. He passed no opinion except to say, 'That will be inexpensive.' The following day, I saw on the 'third copy' that he had sent a letter to all Works for such washers to be put on the brake gear of all classes of engine. No such accidents ever occurred again during my railway career.

About a month later, when the Ministry report came, their recommendation was similar for the other main line railways. My alteration was the result of HNG's training and I heard later that the instruction for me to go to the MOT inquiry was given to Mr Edge by Sir Nigel himself. This is an example of the confidence of HNG in his staff and his method of training. By inviting me into his office as an observer, he had shown me at first hand how to deal with problems and enquiries. His example remained with me for the rest of my railway career.

By now, I had achieved the status of Grade A Draughtsman. I found out by accident that I should have received an increase of salary of £30 per annum. BS saw to it that the increase was put through and I might say that it was very welcome, as I had married on a shoestring. I had to develop HNG's ideas as I had done for TAS and then send them to Doncaster for detailed drawing. Gresley would signify his praise by saying 'That is a fair assessment', accompanied by a twinkle in his eye. The only time that he was likely to be solemn and silent was when a certain Darlington engineer was visiting and Harper would warn us, 'Don't go near Gresley—Thompson is coming!'

Shortly afterwards, HNG asked me to produce rough schemes for a multi-engine locomotive driving through jack-shafts, the schemes for which took a lot of thought. I could find no space below the boiler for separate valve gears, and as Walschaerts valve gear obviously took up too much space, I tried Stephenson gear. Not satisfied, I tried Lentz poppet valves, which BS wanted HNG to fit on the Pacifics.

Both Edward Thompson and BS were keen on the Lentz gear but I did not like it because fixed cams meant that the cut-off could not be finely adjusted. So, unknown to BS, I went to the Great Central section which I knew had locomotives with Caprotti gear. These were the 'B3' 4-6-0s. A search of all the King's Cross records proved fruitless. So I rode on a 'B3' from Marylebone to Sheffield telling HNG that I preferred the Caprotti gear. However, he gave the go-ahead for Thompson to fit the Lentz gear on the 'D49s' at Darlington where I was sent to ride and report. I called them the 'Grasshoppers' because they seemed to 'jump' and were very rough riding.

Another look at my mechanical firing designs did not inspire a way of placing coal in the back corners of the Gresley Pacific wide Wootton firebox, which I knew from footplate experience to be essential for efficient steaming. But further research ceased on the outbreak of World War 2.

4.   The War Years

AS King's Cross station was an obvious target for enemy bombers, the entire office staff was evacuated to Doncaster, except for Sir Nigel, with his Chief Clerk and BS, who set up an office in HNG's home at Watton-at-Stone in Hertfordshire. After about three months of travelling up and down the country from Doncaster to King's Cross, which I thought was a dreadful waste of time, it was decided that I should not be separated from BS. Consequently, I moved back to King's Cross, where I was alone in the large office building.

BS contacted me by phone to send things out for both HNG and himself and the clerical staff at Doncaster requested files and papers from the Filing Room. Therefore, I learned the filing system and, naturally, I looked at my own file as I was interested in the report of the interview at the end of my apprenticeship! It just said, 'Not to be watched'—what it meant, I did not know. On the side of the report was a typewritten word which I could not understand, so I got someone to translate. It simply said, 'Persistence'.

Then I was involved in measuring up and planning office space at Bush Hill Park, in the large house previously owned by Maynard, the sweet manufacturer. The evacuated staff returned from Doncaster and I shared an office with Leslie Nicholson again, my counterpart on the carriage side.

While at Bush Hill Park, Sir Nigel told Mr Edge to ask me to estimate the total tonnage of steel required in the following year for the LNER. This was a most unusual request as the weight of locomotives and machinery naturally included brass and other alloys. I did not know where to start but I had to do it. Mr Edge had no idea either. So I got out the files detailing the acquisition of machinery in previous years, but they merely gave the cost! I went over to Stratford Works and consulted the Chief Draughtsman, Mr Bristow, and his assistant, Sidney King. I asked their help in estimating the weight of steel **only** in the various types of machines. It was virtually an impossibility.

I realised that nobody would be able to criticise me as nobody else knew the answer anyway! So I estimated the amount of steel likely to be required for locomotives, carriages, coaling plant, turntables and the like, eventually arriving at a figure for which I had little confidence. However, Sir Nigel accepted it without question. I later discovered that my estimate had been used for the other three companies too! They had been asked for estimates but could provide no answers, but my training under Sir Nigel had given me the confidence to attempt to find out. Even so, I could hardly call it more than a guess. During the war, the four railway companies pooled their resources in the interests of the war effort, which was how my estimate came to be used for the whole railway network!

Rupert Hart-Davies took me out to Gresley's house at Watton several times. He had influence with an Army General who persuaded HNG to release him for the Forces. Thinking that I was wasting my time at Bush Hill Park, I requested that I could be released to join the Forces too. Sir Nigel refused my request. He rang me up and said, 'No, you can't go to the Forces. There's more important work for you to do in this country.'

Two weeks later, he sent me to Dukinfield Factory which had previously been the Great Central Carriage Works. HNG's instructions to me were, 'You will find the work very different from locomotives but do what you can—plan and equip the whole works.'

Dukinfield

My brief was to convert the old carriage works into a factory for the manufacture of cartridge cases and shells. The machinery was to be supplied by the Ministry of Armament Production (MAP). In the middle of bombing, I left my luggage in the driver's room and went out to my digs at Openshaw. From a canal bridge, I looked over a deserted Manchester which was ablaze with burning buildings —it was bright enough to read the paper. Used to the London Blitz as I was, I had adopted a fatalistic attitude to life and could not help wondering where the fire-fighters were.

Although I felt that I was doing useful work at Dukinfield, conditions of work were far from pleasant. Not only that, but the Superintendent was the most objectionable man that I have ever met and he had the reputation of giving foremen the sack! (I remembered him from Doncaster, where he would not pay his PPA fees!) He was an absolute bully and, within a few weeks of my arrival, he had already sacked three people. One day he said, 'That's not how I told you to do it. You're sacked.' I simply ignored him and carried on planning the factory.

Three months later, the 'bully' asked me to design a tool in such a way that I knew it would break immediately on use, so I designed one that would be satisfactory. Immediately he reacted, 'I've told you before. You're sacked! So I turned to him and said, 'Sir Nigel sent me here and I'll go when he asks me to go back and I will not go for anybody else.' He was shaking with fury. He could not even point to something as his hand was trembling!

Unfortunately, in 1941 Sir Nigel died. I was completely stunned and felt that the bottom of my world had dropped away. HNG was such a great engineer and he was so pleasant to work for that I felt him to be irreplaceable. The greater part of the equipment of the cartridge case factory was finished. However, I had been directed to equip the factory completely, so I continued.

With the help of my assistant, Eric Trotter, I set up a drawing office on the ground floor. From below ground level, we had to remove two enormous Lancashire boilers. I superintended the job and Gresley's training from running shed days helped me in this task.

One evening, I went down to a foreman's office and found the 'bully' inside, knowing that he had been removed from his position of Manager. He pointed to me with a trembling finger and said, 'As for you, you're responsible for this.' So I quietly replied, 'Yes, sir and proud of it.' Altogether he had sacked seven foremen and they had taken notice until I arrived and ignored him, telling them to do likewise. I had no directive to do this—my duties were purely technical—but this was wartime and his attitude was inexcusable. My time with HNG had given me the necessary confidence to act in the best interests of the railway and the country.

The next Superintendent was Frankie Carr from Stratford Works, who was a most likeable man. J.S. Jones, whom I knew well, came as his assistant. Jones had a sense of humour which came to the fore one day when he put up a notice in the passageway leading to the ladies' conveniences. It read, 'Is Your Journey Really Necessary?', and was similar to notices posted in trains. We had noticed that the girls usually went in pairs to the 51-seater, as we termed the ample accommodation. No doubt they felt that there was safety in numbers!

After the shell forge was complete and the end of my work was in sight, Frankie Carr sent for me and said, 'Bannister, your work here is about finished. What you can do now, I don't know, but I can offer you two posts. You can either go back to your old job which is now at Doncaster under Sir Nigel's successor, Edward Thompson, or you can go to Gorton Works as Senior

Draughtsman.' Knowing the uncomfortable time that BS was having at Doncaster and being acquainted with Edward Thompson, I decided to go to Gorton, although not wishing to return to the position of draughtsman. Frankie Carr told me that Freddie Harrison was an up and coming man and that he was well-liked. My wife and I had found very comfortable accommodation at Hollingworth and as Gorton was nearby a removal would not be necessary.

Gorton

I was very happy at Gorton. As the Chief Draughtsman was often away, and known jokingly as the 'Minister of Outings', I had to take over his duties. I remembered him from Doncaster. The foremen soon started coming to the Drawing Office and dealing with me as if I were the Chief. Unfortunately, I received no more pay!

Gorton Works was making two-inch U.P. shells for anti-aircraft rocket guns, the housing of which was to be installed on merchant ships. There was a problem with the design of the casing for the gun. Ministry drawings were no help and neither were those from Doncaster; so I scratched my head to see what I could come up with. I decided to use a mathematical calculation rather than the graphical method. My results were completely different from the other two! When Jim Vardy developed the plate from my drawing he discovered that it was just one eighth of an inch out on one of the curves. As a result, Frederick Harrison (JFH to us) was delighted that Gorton was the first works in the country to be able to produce the gun casing and copies of the drawing were sent to Doncaster and many other works.

A week or two later, Freddie Harrison came to me in the office and said, 'Would you like to go on the management, Bannister?' I replied that I would. He said, 'You start on Monday', so I said, 'Does that mean I get a rise?' He said, 'Yes. You'll be the third manager in the works and your duties will be engine output. I did this job years ago on the Lancashire & Yorkshire Railway but I'm not going to tell you how to do it. You develop your own methods.' I said to JFH, 'This is a bit of a tall order.' He said, 'Never mind, you have a go. You will receive a salary increase of £350 per annum.' This brought me up to the same salary level as BS used to have in London.

The Ministry had decided that railways were to have first priority for steel now as it was important to ensure that the munitions were kept moving instead of being stockpiled for lack of transport.

I decided that the only way to progress the work was to visit all the foremen at least twice a day. With the help of Jim Vardy, the chairman of the foremen's committee, I found them most helpful and cooperative.

Ironically, it was the highest paid foreman of the Erecting Shop, Tracey, who was the most obstructive in estimating the proposed output for the week ahead. The assistant foreman, Tommy Williams, was just the opposite. I asked him to introduce me to all the Erecting Shop chargehands to whom I spoke in a friendly way, following HNG's example. The shop was rather disorganised and I advised Tommy that reorganisation was necessary to get the most efficient output. All the chargehands freely explained the details of their work.

New gantries were needed for the Boiler Shop and a young boilersmith cooperated throughout the erection and timing by stop-watch to fix the piecework prices. I had a plan of the Erecting Shop divided into bays and locomotive positions, so that I could check the overall position of the output. Tracey continued to be surly and uncooperative. To see what repaired components had been delivered from the feeding shops, I had to observe a mixed pile at the top of the Shop. The engine parts were already stamped with the engine number, so I asked the foreman of the feeding shops to arrange for them to be placed at the top of the pit where the engine was placed. The labourer's chargehand improved upon this by placing the parts next to the appropriate frame.

When I had been to the Machine Shop chargehand of the valve motion gang, I observed him consulting the back of a cigarette packet. I noticed his W-shaped marks and asked him to explain. He told me that it recorded the work in progress. The first stroke of the W meant material arrived, the second stroke meant work in progress, the third stroke meant no snags and the fourth stroke meant work completed and sent to the Erecting Shop. I asked him if he would mind if I adopted his idea for all the shops. He agreed and I asked the Joiner's Foreman to make boards lined in white paint for all chargehands. Every gang had a board with a 'W' for each component and I introduced the idea of marking with a short line to be drawn across the relevant stroke whenever a snag occurred.

The chargehands cooperated splendidly in keeping their chalk marks up to date. Thus I could see at a glance the state of progress at all levels without interrupting their work. I had a master plan based on the 'W' and dealt with their snags as they arose. As a result, the output started to increase immediately. It also saved me a lot of time. The whole staff knew that I made my rounds at least twice a day and, apart from a friendly greeting, spoke only for the exchange of information. I kept the chargehands informed of the situation and cut through the bureaucracy of the Chief Clerk to make sure that they had proper manilla-backed notebooks and pencils!

Cooperation extended to men of the lowest grades. One day I moved aside to let a labourer pass with a barrow load of repaired components along the side of a pit to a locomotive frame. He said, 'Can I speak to you, Mr Bannister?' 'Of course, certainly. Are you in trouble?' was my reply. He said, 'When I push a barrow along, I take too much time lifting the pipes over the barrow. If we could have little bridges over the pipes, I could do it much quicker.' Why I had not thought of it myself, I do not know. I thanked him for the idea and rang Harry Barker, the Boiler Shop foreman, and told him to burn up some scrap boiler barrel plates at a suitable length and width for every pit and, if possible, for every engine. This was done by the next day. There was a labour shortage everywhere and this saved ten labourers. To my regret, I could not find the man again to thank him.

There was almost a walk-out over a mistake by J.S. Jones, who came as Assistant Works Manager. Jess Turner, the smithy foreman, came to see me in great agitation as the men in the Drop-Stamp Shop and smithy had threatened to stop work. It turned out that J.S. Jones had seen the men sitting outside on a pile of steel bars and spoke sharply to them for wasting time. I walked past the men with a smile and said, 'Having a cooler?' before going on to the smithy and my office. Jess rang almost at once to say that the men were back at their jobs. I went and explained to Jones the necessity of a cooler for such hot work. Jones went at once to apologise to Jess and the men.

Every Friday I held a Locomotive Foremen's meeting to discuss the output plans. Tracey tried to dictate which engines should be on the list. Knowing the overall position in all the shops, I did not always agree with him. Albert Simpson, who had replaced Jones (who had gone on to Stratford), agreed with me after consulting my progress board. I had set this up in his office so that he could see the position at a glance. Engine numbers were written in Indian ink on square plastic sheets to denote work in progress, while yellow triangles indicated 'leftover' engines on which work was not completed.

The output continued to rise and so did the piecework earnings of the men. However, I noticed that they were beginning to show signs of tiredness. I proposed that the whole works should close down for one weekend in three except for the necessary maintenance. Harrison was very doubtful but agreed on condition that the present output was maintained. I spoke to the chargehands who were keen to try it. I felt that the men had reached a stage where constant work meant that output had reduced.

At first we were only just one engine short, but the following week the men recovered the lost output and, from then onwards, we had the same figure every week and the men were looking much more pleased. My wife appreciated the break too! They did not lose anything by it because the piecework prices depended on the output and yet they had gained a free weekend. So Harrison was quite satisfied. I called to see the men on both day and night shifts and they thanked me for arranging the weekend off.

A lighter moment was provided when JFH told me to meet Wilfred Pickles and his wife Mabel who were coming from the BBC to report to the newspapers on the theme of 'Women at War'. The party arrived and told me that they required photogenic women to illustrate the article. I chose a tall, strong blonde young woman who drove an overhead travelling crane and happened to be a good crane driver! This suited them very well and an engine was lifted. Then the reporters requested women doing heavy work, so I took them to the Drop-Stamp Shop. They went behind my back and posed a young coloured girl standing by an anvil, holding a sledge hammer in the air. She never hit anything! An attempt to pose a girl near men pouring molten iron failed as she was afraid, so they posed the first blonde holding open the smokebox door!

After about a year, JFH saw me in the works and we went round together. He went everywhere and asked me many questions, not only about my own sphere of influence. However, I was able to answer all his questions as I had kept an inconspicuous eye on Albert Simpson's duties when he had been away. Then Freddie turned to me outside the Iron Foundry and said, 'Because I have not been to see you, don't think that you've been forgotten. It is just that everything is going so well that there has been no need to speak to you.' I went home and had an easy night's sleep!

The next day I went to JFH's office and asked if he was there. He saw me at once and I told him about Tracey but added that he was a capable foreman and that I did not wish him any harm. Freddie said, 'I know all about him and I am shifting him to another post at the same salary, for he means well but he just can't get on with other people.' The post was allocated to the assistant foreman from the Machine Shop.

Following Tracey's removal, the output continued to rise and with the increase in earnings from piecework, I became liked throughout the works. They responded to my friendly attitude. Freddie Harrison saw me again after only a month and said, 'Up again, Bannister. I doubt whether the Gresley training has reached its peak yet!' I replied, 'Perhaps not but I may wish to see you first. There are limits to my efforts.' He replied, 'Keep on with your usual methods, they have given me another engine.' When last I saw him it had gone up from nine to ten but I was aiming for eleven.

Then there was trouble in the Brass Foundry. Harrison was very angry as he said, 'Bannister, you are slipping. I will not have the output held up for a silly thing like a washout plug!' Rather crest-fallen, I went to Albert to see if he would mind my encroaching on his territory. He backed me up. I saw Foreman Barber and obtained a pattern, which was old and dilapidated. I showed the pattern maker the necessary alterations. The moulder was not there. The next day he was still missing and despite a note left with his clock-on card, still only produced a part mould. In desperation I finished it off myself. The men were amazed as I used the swan-neck trowel, which is the most difficult to use. I thanked Gresley in my mind for the thorough apprenticeship that I had received at Doncaster! Eventually, the man was removed as his time-keeping record was atrocious. JFH came to our usual meeting in Simpson's office and said, 'A bit more of Gresley training. You have done it again, Bannister.' I always got the thumbs-up in the Foundry after that, as they were not delayed and their piecework earnings rose accordingly.

There was an amusing incident when the new Works Manager, 'Uncle George' Caster, came from the Great Eastern. Gorton quite liked him but as a southerner nobody could understand him (including Albert). He was very uncommunicative and made everyone stand in front of his desk. On the wall behind his head, he had a large framed enlargement of 'A3' *Felstead,* which was always at an alarming angle; this seemed out of character with his fastidious nature.

Then he asked for his office to be cleaned while he was away. I arranged this and carefully levelled the enlargement. I asked the Chief Clerk to ensure that it was not due to vibration. When 'Uncle George' returned, I looked at the picture and then at him. There was a twinkle in his eye. From that moment, he always asked me to take a chair at his side and we were on excellent terms. But the picture stayed crooked!

Because of the shortage of fitters during the war, JFH sent me to

Derby to borrow some men. The Works Manager commented that the output at Gorton was small compared to the Derby output. I pointed out that he had more men and said, 'At Gorton, we have less than 100 fitters. Your output per man is roughly 50% less than the figure for Gorton.' He lent us five fitters who were good men in their particular sphere but they were all divided into work squads at Derby. At Gorton the fitters did anything and would tackle any job. The Derby men could not compete and asked to return home as they felt they were not earning their money.

Then I had a disagreement with JFH. Edward Thompson had asked him to build some boilers for 'B17' 4-6-0s, a job which the Gorton boilermakers did not like. This was done without my knowledge and, as the output was falling, I took the men off the 'B17s'. Harrison sent for me to enquire why the work had stopped. I stood up to him and pointed out, 'Well, sir, you put me in charge of the engine output which is the bread and butter of Gorton.' He was rather annoyed but I went on, 'If you had done it in the right way, you would have got both your engine output and your boiler. You will get your boiler as I know you wish to be the first to produce one.' He said, 'Well, Bannister, all right. I take your point but I will not lose a single engine on the output. That is, as you say, the bread and butter of Gorton.' I said, 'If you'd done it in the right way, you wouldn't have lost anything at all and you'll get your boiler.'

I called on the chairman of the Works Committee and explained the position. He suggested that I ask the men if they would work overtime in order to keep our schedule and get the 'B17' boiler out. The men agreed on condition that their wives were informed. I asked other men who were their neighbours to let their wives know and, as a result, JFH got his wish.

Tommy Williams from the Erecting Shop showed me three 15-inch naval guns complete with the breeches which were hidden under the shop floor. I found some heavy blocks of what turned out to be tin and a stock of engine parts there. Whilst I was on fire-watch, we moved the valuable tin to a cellar under JFH's office. This was our secret source of tin, which was in short supply and JFH did not know that he was sitting on it!

We managed to double the output of repaired engines. The men were delighted because the piecework went sky-high. We were dealing with 'Director' class 4-4-0s. They were good-paying engines as far as piecework was concerned and, in fact, were the best 4-4-0s on the LNER. Their only fault was that because of their Belpaire firebox they did not fit in with Gresley's idea of aesthetics. The most popular locomotive was the '04' 2-8-0 because it was easy to work on and brought good piecework prices.

As we were having difficulty with getting supplies from the Stores, I took matters into my own hands. There was a shortage of four-square files and the Stores said that the 18in files were unobtainable. So I went into Manchester and ordered some from an ironmongers! JFH was informed as I had by-passed the Stores. So I explained that they were essential for axleboxes and that output was my concern. JFH said, 'Quite right, Bannister. I'd have done the same myself.'

At the next foremen's meeting in Harrison's office, they complained that they had difficulty in controlling the Stores. I said to JFH, 'The whole of the Shop Stores needs reorganising.' I told him that they were in an absolute muddle. JFH said, 'I'll take your word for that, Bannister. Right. Come off the engine repairs progress and I'll leave you to reorganise the whole of the Stores procedure. You thought of it, now you do it!'

I decided to erect racks for storage and establish a proper system so that you could see at a glance what was available. The shortage of materials meant that it was decided that the racks should be made of old boiler tubes. I immediately encountered labour problems. The welding was claimed to be the work of boilersmiths, coppersmiths, fitters and the smithy! So I decided to design a rack which included every trade. When I showed the drawings to the Works Committee, they said that nobody could do the whole of the racks. I replied, 'I know they can't. You have your trades to consider but the designer is really the boss!' The meeting ended with everyone thoroughly amused and it was agreed that any trade could make the racks according to the availability of labour.

Ian Cookman replaced me on the job of managing the engine output. He was well-qualified but not very experienced and so output dropped. Albert Simpson, with whom I remained on friendly terms, asked me to intervene. When I consulted my progress board, I noticed that an 'N1' had failed to arrive, so I rang Trafford Park to see if they would like one to be repaired quickly. It arrived that evening. Meanwhile I had a quiet word with Ian. He was not a bad sort but a bit of a twerp! When he got married we filled his cases with confetti and discovered that when he shook it out of the window, a cross-wind blew it back into the adjacent room occupied by his wife!

When the Stores were reorganised, I began to get restless. I wanted to make more progress in my career. I had asked Gresley to sponsor me for Corporate Membership of the Institute of

Mechanical Engineers which he had declined to do at the time, saying that I was a bit young and needed more experience, including the control of men. Although I was working as third manager and I had a lot of responsibility and was accepted by all the men, the Works Manager was nominally in control. I had asked JFH if he thought I had any chance of getting my A.M.I.Mech.E. and he replied that as a Gresley trained man, even he could not get Thompson to sponsor him. 'Uncle George' said he would gladly second me but Thompson would have to sponsor me.

The end of the war was in sight. I felt that Gresley had been right and that I had contributed more to the war effort by remaining on the railway than I could have done in the Forces. However, men were returning to their own jobs and I could not see a future at Gorton. So I applied for the position advertised as Motive Power Superintendent at Hornsey. JFH tried to persuade me to remain with him but, when I explained my feelings, he passed on my application with reluctance.

It was with some regret that I left Gorton having been successful in my job application. JFH was a good leader with an easy and friendly attitude. Like HNG, he was the boss but his position was never resented. I had found the men to be good workers and friendly with it. Even the women were friendly. There was an excellent tracer called Elsie who took pity on me on the day I had all my teeth out and returned to work. She introduced me to 'pobs' from the canteen, which turned out to be warm bread and milk. This concoction enabled me to continue my rounds. So it was with mixed feelings that I left the North.

5.   Shedmaster at Hornsey

ALTHOUGH my new job was completely different from being in a major works, I thought that with Gresley's training behind me I could tackle the Running Department management quite well. My wife and I moved back into our London home which we had let out during our time in the North and we prepared to resume our lives in peacetime. However, my first impressions of Hornsey were far from peaceful. I was instructed from Doncaster to report to the Shed at 9 a.m. and duly arrived to find that my office had been demolished the previous week by an engine which had overrun the turntable. The shed was in an awful mess and my predecessor, who had moved on to become the Assistant Running Superintendent at King's Cross, arrived to inform me that I should be with Frampton, the District Running Superintendent.

When I entered Frampton's office that afternoon, he was rather aggressive. He said, 'Well, you've come to take over Hornsey have you, Bannister? I don't know you, I don't know anything about you and I do not want you! What have you got to say to that?' I replied, 'Well, sir, it's up to me to make you change your mind.' He said, 'Well, you go to Hornsey and see what you think then. It is the shed in the District which gives me the most trouble.'

With this challenge in mind, I returned to Hornsey to see what I could make of the place. The Chief Clerk was on leave and his relief could only find me a desk in the General Office. Obviously, this was unsatisfactory as there was no privacy for confidential staff interviews, so I looked round the shed and found a disused room under the old manual coaling-plant. It was filthy and had no windows but at least it had a fireplace and was private. I arranged for it to be cleaned up and set up my office in there.

Then I organised a major cleaning up operation around the shed. The place had a derelict air as if nobody took a pride in their work. There were great piles of ashes which had been thrown out of the engine ashpans just anywhere so that the driver and fireman could get home quickly. Everything was just as it had been left after the war.

About a month later, Mr Frampton and his Chief Clerk, Cork, came to my office and Frampton said, 'Well, Bannister, you've made yourself reasonably comfortable.' I explained the need for privacy to discuss personal matters. He replied, 'One thing I'll say for you. It's the first time since I've been in charge of the District that I've been able to get round Hornsey without mountaineering over the ashes! We both walked round with the greatest of ease. Now see what you can do with the staff and smarten them up as you've done with the shed; then I shall change my mind.'

I found the NUR men much more cooperative than their ASLEF counterparts. So I set out to work with the NUR men. Six months after my arrival, the Local Departmental Committee (LDC) meeting took place in my newly rebuilt office. There was an instruction that the Shedmaster could not see the LDC on his own. In ignorance of this, I arranged that I would hold monthly meetings with them in my office. The Chief Clerk, Arthur Smith, who was trying to be helpful, told me about it and left the letter on my desk. Without reading it, I threw it on the fire when he had gone. As I told Arthur, it was impossible to deal with the men's problems unless we met face to face to discuss them before they got out of hand.

Thereafter, each month I met the LDC without fail. They made no difficulty, simply asking if they could adjourn to the corridor for voting. I agreed and the procedure was resolved. They even got me some carpet for my office! I always tried to do my best for the mutual interests of the men and the railway as HNG would have done. The only thing that I queried in their voting system was that the men were told how to place their votes. I said, 'This is a free country. Do you consider that for people to be instructed on how to vote is in accordance with democracy?' They replied that they did not like it either but that it was a trade union directive!

On looking round the shed, I was surprised at the number of women workers. Arthur Smith informed me that they were conscripted cleaners and that they caused a lot of disruption of the shed with the drivers and firemen. I soon found that they were a nuisance. I went to see the women in their pleasant mess room and discovered that they did not want to be there at all. So I told Arthur to give them all two weeks' notice. He pointed out that I shouldn't do that without Liverpool Street knowing. So I said, 'Arthur, to hell with Liverpool Street! Give them their notice.' I went to see the manager at the Labour Exchange who agreed that there was no longer any need for conscription. The ladies were glad to leave and their former mess room was converted into a Mutual Improvement

Class for firemen!

My regular meetings with the men paid dividends as I was able to get to know them and they realised that they could always come and see me with their personal problems. I developed a fatherly attitude towards them as I well knew the problems involved in working on the footplate. When I was having problems with the late return of engines to the shed from general traffic which prevented me from meeting Hornsey's traffic requirements, I spoke to several drivers who complained that they were delayed on the way back to the shed. Finding out that the delays had no discernible pattern, I sent out a young fireman to see if he could find the cause. He did a splendid job and I made a graph of his findings.

The next thing that happened was that the Yardmaster from Wood Green arrived to complain of spying! I quietly told him, 'Yes, I was trying to find out why my engines were returning late so often. I was not spying on you. I was merely trying to improve the general working of the line.' He said, 'I see, you weren't spying on us?' I said, 'No. My responsibility is to work over the lines from Hornsey and I do not wish to send my engines out late and delay your workings.' He became less aggressive and I showed him my graphs. We finished up as friends and he promised to do all in his power to help!

Then there was a fatal accident to one of my firemen in Oakleigh Park Tunnel. Mr Frampton rang up and asked me to go to the inquest at Harringay with him. I joined Frampton in the Waiting Hall and listened to the proceedings. When the coroner, Colonel Lane, said, 'Can anybody give me a reason why this man should be in the tunnel at that time of night?' I spoke up, much to Frampton's surprise, and said, 'Yes, sir, I can give a possible reason.' So he invited me to sit beside him and said, 'Speak loudly and address the whole court.' I said, 'It's very simple. The fireman was standing for examination to be passed out as a driver and, to be a driver, one must be completely aware of all the signals. I think, sir, he could have been out at that time of night to improve his knowledge.'

The coroner then gave his final direction. 'You heard the evidence. Your verdict should not be suicide or anything adverse to this man. I direct the court that it should not be anything but either accidental death or excess of zeal.' The jury returned a verdict of accidental death. When I left the court with Frampton, he said, 'Well done, Bannister. He was married, I think? Good. It will mean that any insurance or union payments will go to his widow.'

The men were all very pleased with the verdict and, as a result, they were even more cooperative. One of the rules was that each locomotive should go out with a bucket of tools so that the footplatemen could do certain small jobs when required. As there was a postwar shortage of tools, I asked the LDC to suspend the rule for a short time to give the shed a chance to obtain stock. They readily agreed and, after retiring to the corridor, asked if I could do it in three months. I told them that I hoped to do it in less time and they said, 'Rule suspended from tomorrow', and put up a notice to that effect.

I was fortunate in knowing the right foreman, Brooks, from my Doncaster Crimpsall days. He agreed to supply me with all the tools I needed and I acquired a set for every engine. Then the rule was re-adopted. When Frampton found out, he asked me if I could get some tools for him, too! Unfortunately, my messenger died soon after while I was on a course at Darlington. I had great difficulty with the Liverpool Street Staff Clerk over his replacement, but finally succeeded. Frampton commented, 'You Works people are teaching us a thing or two!'

Gradually, Frampton became more friendly. He started to send Pacifics and other large engines for servicing at Hornsey so as to relieve King's Cross Shed. We had a 65ft diameter turntable and a Mitchell mechanical coaling-plant. Hornsey Shed was slowly building up a reputation for reliability. Frampton asked me to recruit drivers and firemen for King's Cross as he had difficulty getting suitable men. One reason for this became apparent when I relieved at Top Shed for two weeks. I found that my predecessor here had taken his untidy ways with him and the place was a mess. After I had been there a week, the Fitting Shop foreman asked if I was taking over. He commented, 'It's a pity it isn't permanent!'

Because of our increasing efficiency, Hornsey was asked to stage the coal consumption trials which had been unsuccessfully tried using King's Cross Shed. Inspector Dixon from Liverpool Street came to outline his plan which used 'O2' three-cylinder 2-8-0s. This involved repairing the old coaling stage. The men were not keen on climbing up to a height, so I climbed up myself as I had done once before at Doncaster. I suggested that a rope be fixed at the edge of the walkway to warn the men if they got too near. As ever, there is nothing like example and the stage was repaired in time. The trials were an immediate success and we were proud of our part in them.

In the early days at Hornsey, pilfering was a problem. So, against the advice of my Chief Clerk, I put up a notice stating, 'I realise the difficulty of purchasing engineering equipment. If you wish to take out a parcel from the shed, please ask me for a note giving you authorisation.' There was a shortage of materials in the shops, hence the problem. I went to Wood Green Police Station and showed them a copy of the notice. They had been stopping men regularly. Everyone thought that I was asking for trouble but, when I asked Dick Deeds, the storesman, a few months later, he told me that it had stopped completely.

Part of my solution to the Shed's problems was to go out on the footplate as often as practicable. In this way, I got to know all the men well and they could speak to me informally, allowing me to gauge the feelings of the men on a number of topics. I also learnt the various lines worked by Hornsey crews. It was interesting to ride over these routes which included crossing to Southern and Great Western territory and allowed me to observe their different signalling practices. Driver Freckleton reckoned that he knew Southern lines down to the South Coast and he made a plan of all the workings from Hornsey. I travelled on the footplate from Moorgate to Clapham Junction, Hither Green and Herne Hill.

This travelling paid off when I had to attend derailments and other accidents. There came an urgent phone call one day from the Running Foreman to say that an 'N2' returning from Clapham had been derailed in 'The Hole'. This was the section in tunnel leading to King's Cross Suburban Station from the Widened Lines and Moorgate. I immediately commandeered a Hornsey 'N1' and went to the derailed 'N2' and found that Driver Morris was finding great difficulty in breathing. In fact, I found that the only way to breathe was to go down on all fours and keep my nose close to the ground. I directed him out of the tunnel and used my breakdown whistle to summon the 'N1'. Then I got on the 'N2' footplate from which the wagons had been uncoupled and gave the signal to the 'N1'. Between us we got out of 'The Hole'.

When Driver Morris returned the next morning for his rostered turn, he came to my office and said, 'Mr Bannister, I can't go on that turn again. I daren't go down "The Hole" again.' Realising that if he did not go on the turn immediately, he would destroy the whole of his career, I was firm and insisted that he must go. However, I told him that when he returned from the Southern, I would be waiting for him at Farringdon station and that I would go through 'The Hole' with him back to Hornsey. I duly went to Farringdon at the right time and Morris went through the station, waving as he went through 'The Hole' on his way home. The following morning he reported for his turn in the normal way but called in the office and said, 'You were right, Mr Bannister, but if you had not been on Farringdon platform, I daren't have come through!'

The most interesting work at Hornsey was with the breakdown gang headed by Brooks, who was excellent and showed me many dodges. We had many breakdowns to attend, mainly of goods trains. We only had a 15 ton capacity steam crane but the men were experts with hydraulic jacks. On one occasion we 'threw' an 'N2' which had ploughed into loose earth at Ferme Park so that it landed with all wheels on the rails! I wouldn't have thought it possible, but Brooks showed me that by packing up the jacks gradually with blocks of wood as the jacks were pumped almost to maximum height, they eventually tipped it over, throwing the engine upright. It was a highly skilled operation.

One day, Frampton rang up to say that an engine was derailed in the cutting known as the 'Khyber Pass' at Wood Green on the line leading from the main line to the Hertford Loop. He said, 'I can't get the breakdown cranes to the engine. It is leaning against the side of a cutting. Your gang at Hornsey is expert with hydraulic jacks, so send them out.' We rerailed the engine and quickly pulled it away with another. King's Cross could have done it more quickly with their 45 ton crane if they had been able to reach it, but we were always pleased to get one up on the Top Shed!

Brooks was a good fitter and deputised for the boilersmith after he had suffered an accident when he was maintaining the water-softener. He could turn his hand to most things, having served his time at Doncaster. There were many accidents, one of which happened when a red flag restricting the line near the Mitchell coaling-plant blew down in a gale. The Ministry Inspector who came to investigate was my old friend, C.H. Hewison, from our Doncaster days!

Frampton summoned us out one day to deal with a derailed 'V2' 2-6-2 at Hatfield on the East Coast main line. Although a 45 ton Ransomes crane had been sent via Hertford, and the 45 ton Peterborough crane had been sent to work from the north of the smash, Frampton said that neither would be able to get near because of the splintered coaches. Fortunately, the train was made up of empty stock and the only 'casualty' was the corpse of an old lady whose coffin had shattered in the derailment.

When we arrived, the Operating Superintendent was there with the relatives and insisted that the corpse must not be damaged any more. The Hornsey Breakdown van approached first from the south containing our usual emergency supply of biscuits as we never knew when we would get a meal on this job and I once survived for two days on biscuits. I looked at the wreckage and whistled my men to start clearing the debris. The corpse was very far gone and lay under a carriage bogie. We tried to lift the wrecked bogie and shattered wooden coach. The presence of the corpse and a rail which was bent like a hairpin through the up side and out of the window on the down side, seriously held things up. Brooks and I decided on our plan of action. The men were clearing the debris of a number of coaches towards the south. Then we started to clear the wood from the bogie—all with the Hornsey 15 ton steam crane. Once cleared, we started on the bogie. I whistled up the ambulance men and we carefully slid a carriage panel under the body without causing any more harm. Frampton stood well away on the up side—and I do not blame him!

I walked along to the undamaged engine in front of the wrecked train and Frampton tore his shoe badly on the ballast. He was rather concerned because there was still rationing and he was short of clothing coupons. I said, 'That is why you have supplementary coupons.' Mr Musgrave, the Running Superintendent, commiserated with Frampton who had just informed me that the Staff Clerk at HQ denied staff the extra coupons. They were amazed when I told them I received them. So I told them to consult the manager of the Labour Exchange to make the decision about such matters and referred them to the relevant document. Both men phoned me the next morning to tell me that they had got them! So much for the assumed power of Chief Clerks and their ilk.

I happened to mention to Frampton one day that my wife and I had enjoyed the opera at Sadler's Wells the previous night. He replied, 'You're supposed to be on call 24 hours a day, seven days a week. How can you be called if you are at the theatre?' I told him that I often went with my wife. 'I've made arrangements with the theatre to bill me on the stage if there is a call-out and I've directed the Post Office to divert all calls to the theatre.' Frampton looked and said, 'You bugger! I've told you that you've taught us a thing or two in the Motive Power Depot that you've learnt from the Works.' In fact, all the theatres were very cooperative and I've been billed out from both Covent Garden and the Albert Hall. Obviously, without this arrangement, I would have had a very restricted social life. Gresley had taught me how to find a solution to problems!

After two years of being on call constantly, I phoned JFH and said, 'You were right, sir, I don't like Running Department work.' He replied, 'I've no vacancies at Cowlairs, Bannister, so I can't help you as much as I'd like to.' I was told that there was no need to move to Scotland as I could become shedmaster at King's

Cross in the near future. I pointed out that not only was I after more experience, but more money!

About a month later, the phone range and it was the well-known voice of JFH. He told me that there was a vacancy at Cowlairs for a Budgetary Control Officer. He said, 'Bannister, I want you to come here on Monday morning first thing for interview. It will not be held by me but by some consultants brought in by Sir Ronald Matthews.'

Unfortunately, a sleeper could not be obtained as Army officers had taken them all. So I travelled overnight to Scotland, sitting up in a corner of a first-class compartment. When I got to Cowlairs, I reported to JFH who sent me across the works to the Accountants offices. He said, 'They will interview you and, I warn you Bannister, eight people sent up for interview have been turned down!' So I crossed the works with mixed feelings after my long journey. The consultants, Robson and Morrow, gave me a real grilling until 4 p.m. They announced at the outset that it was easier to teach accountancy to an engineer than vice-versa, which was a crumb of comfort! By the end of the interview, I felt like a wet rag. However, I revived when I went to say goodbye to JFH. He said, 'Hello, Bannister, when are you starting?' I said, 'You don't mean to say I've got the job?' He said, 'You have, I knew you would.'

6.   New Directions

JFH, knowing my ambition to become a Works Manager one day, told me that Sir Ronald Matthews had decreed that all WMs must in future have budgetary cost-control experience and training. So I settled down in a bed-sitter near Cowlairs to benefit from this opportunity. Once I had put the basic ideas into everyday English, I found that my experience of studying piecework and bonus schemes under Sir Nigel at King's Cross was invaluable.

Then, the Robson and Morrow representative asked me to explain the scheme to the next group which came to the lecture room. I was scared stiff for I had never spoken publicly before but, when I realised that I was the only person who knew what it was all about, my confidence grew.

I found the masses of figures rather boring, but realised that a thorough knowledge of budgetary control would mean that I would be in a position to interpret the needs and possible savings in a works. This complemented my practical engineering experience and I felt better able to advise at all levels as a result. From my large office next to JFH, I conducted many lectures to the Works Committee and salaried staff, including the accountants! I tried to explain things to the foremen in a friendly way, as practised by HNG, which I found to be effective even at Cowlairs despite the poor reputation of the works.

After about six months, JFH sent me to Inverurie to help the Works Manager, Lionel Farr, to work out a bonus scheme for the men who were then on day work. The Rowan Formula was in force on instruction from Doncaster. This scheme was resented by the men as it was harder to make more money by extra work than it was on straight piecework. This formula is now illegal and HNG had stopped it in his days on the Great Northern!

Realising that the men in Inverurie blamed Farr and me for the anomaly, I caught the eye of the Works Committee secretary at the next meeting and said pointedly that I would be at Parkhead station the following evening. He got the message and was there so I was able to whisper casually to him where to find the relevant book while I waited for my train to Glasgow. My plan was successful and JFH was able to pass on the men's objections with favourable results.

There was some compensation for being so far from home in the wonderful Scottish scenery. I made use of my free pass to take the McBrayne steamers round the lochs and I had a ride over the Settle and Carlisle line in the snows of 1947, which was a spectacular sight. It reminded me that HNG had a footplate ride over the line on a Compound and was going to arrange a similar treat for me before he died. Gresley was in my thoughts again when I saw the beaver-tail observation car from the 'Coronation' set and remembered Bernard Newsome's struggle to keep the perspex rear windows clean for viewing. As I had assisted him, I knew only too well that dust and grit seemed attracted to the perspex as if my magic! The car was stored in immaculate condition in the Inverurie paint shop.

JFH was sorely missed when he went to Doncaster as Assistant CME. I finished putting in the scheme at Cowlairs under his successor Blair and discovered the reason for the well-known inefficiency of Cowlairs resulted from the men receiving 'out of office' payments rather than make-up or bonus pay. So there was no incentive to work efficiently as their pay was guaranteed!

The consultants taught me that fair dealings were essential if the respect of the men was to be gained. JFH had gained that respect and I hoped to do so by removing anomalies and ensuring a fair day's pay for a fair day's work. As my work at Cowlairs was almost finished and I had grown tired of travelling home to London for weekends, it was a great relief to me when JFH rang me up and informed me that I was to go to Stratford and implement the budgetary cost control scheme at the Stratford Locomotive, Carriage and Temple Mills Wagon Works.

I was not sorry to leave Scotland, despite the acquaintance of some delightful Scots who had been very generous to my wife and I when she visited for holidays. I thanked JFH for my appointment as he told me that he knew that, with my Gresley training, I should pass the interview. However, he could say nothing beforehand as he was obliged to let the clerks have their say on the basis of seniority of service. The consultants had stressed to me that seniority should only be invoked when all other things were equal. I remember Sir Nigel saying the same thing about drivers in the Top Link but, at the time, I had been too young to realise how right he was. I determined to take this advice with me to Stratford.

Stratford

My years at Stratford coincided with the beginning of British Railways. There was not a significant difference from the LNER as there had been cooperation between the railway companies during the war. The Eastern Region covered a large part of the old LNER territory and the personnel operating therein remained unchanged on the whole. The main difference to me was that at last I had obtained membership of the Institute of Mechanical Engineers, thanks to JFH's recommendation. This was just the boost that I needed to my career prospects.

I was pleased to find that my old friend, Norman Newsome, was the Carriage Works Manager at Stratford and it was significant that his Works Committee was the easiest to deal with. He was a very good WM. The Mechancial Engineer, G.C. Gold, was very helpful and the Locomotive Works Manager, J.H.P. Lloyd, whilst taciturn at first, turned out in the end to be equally helpful. It was a large task to implement the Robson and Morrow scheme and gradually I became known as the 'efficiency officer'.

As there was disagreement about the piecework prices, I was asked to work out a scheme. The NUR accepted it and Stratford Works was the first works to be ready to apply the 728 Railway Shopman's National Council Award. The value of the award was a 27½% increase on all piecework prices. We had to wait for three months before the other works were ready. Then my work in budgetary cost control began to decline and I took an interest in the management side of things. The rows of figures began to bore me and, on my trips round the works, I noticed several anomalies which were likely to lead to disputes.

John Lloyd asked me to answer the boilermakers' grievances. With memories of Gorton in mind, I went to investigate. At once, I saw that from the piecework prices the men were desperate for work for there was insufficient input of tenders for repair to enable the men to make enough money. I managed to sort things out and I was very glad of my wide-ranging apprenticeship experience as I was able to appreciate the problems of the various Shops. My boldness at Doncaster in asking Mr Eggleshaw for permission to sample all the different skills had paid off handsomely.

Whilst I was on holiday in Corsica with my wife, there was a fire in the Trimming Shop. My office adjoined it and I returned to find that my office had been burnt down and I had lost everything. Not only had all the work on the 728 award perished but, more importantly to me, I had lost all my locomotive photographs, including a signed photograph of Sir Nigel Gresley, all the records of my earlier training and all my technical training books. I was devastated. As a result of that fire, I am now completely dependent on my memory in setting down my reminiscences.

I was determined to find the cause of the fire which had tragically deprived me of my records of my early Gresley days. I asked for the punch-cards for the day of the fire. As it had taken place during the night, I asked for the watchman's card. Careful scrutiny revealed that punches were missing. The Works Committee were appalled and said that the man should be sacked. That was the finish as far as everybody else was concerned, but I never got over my loss.

Although I had a new office immediately, I never felt the same again at Stratford and, as I was doing an increasing amount of management but without the pay, I decided to look for a more rewarding position. It was not much use to have management status without the relevant pay! Consequently, I applied for the position of District Outdoor Machinery Engineer at King's Cross and I was successful.

District Outdoor Machinery Engineer at King's Cross

This was a most interesting appointment as my duties were so varied and I was able to use all the skills that I had acquired in the course of my career to date. King's Cross was the largest district covering the East Coast main line to Holme, just south of Peterborough, the whole of the eastern corner of England from London to Shoeburyness and to Witham in Essex. I had a large staff and, so that I would not merely be a name to them, I made a practice of visiting somewhere in the district at least once a week in the company of the inspector and sometimes a foreman.

This policy paid off as I got to know as many people as possible and, clearly they felt that they could talk to me. When there was a strike in the district, the District Committee actually came to me to apologise. I knew that they were in the right, but I was having the usual difficulty with bureaucrats who never ventured beyond their desks at headquarters! When I managed to get fair pay for my men and myself, they gave us the Liverpool Street new electrical signalling to install!

Despite this constant battle, I enjoyed my years as DOME, which were challenging professionally. Apart from the Liverpool Street signal controlling, we did extensive work at Temple Mills marshalling yard, installed the express lifts at 222 Marylebone

Road and, naturally enough, there was continual maintenance required for the existing electrical and signal controlling plant. Although I was on constant call, I used my Hornsey technique so that I could enjoy a social life of theatres and concerts.

Just as my career was approaching its climax, I was diagnosed as having DS, or Multiple Sclerosis, as it is now known. It hardly affected me at first and I had been given verbal confirmation of an appointment as manager when it became known to the bureaucrats with whom I had done battle on so many occasions. Unfortunately, I had to have a couple of days off because of a minor ailment and my regular doctor, who had refrained from mentioning the DS on any certificates, was away and the dreaded letters appeared. I had been warned that the illness could affect my career prospects but I was in good health and at first not at all disabled.

The result was that my appointment was not confirmed and I was frustrated in further attempts to obtain a recognised post. My thoughts on the railway at the time are obviously unprintable, especially since I knew a civil engineer in my district with DS who could hardly walk and who was collected by a pool car! I was told by several people that I had made enemies in the ranks of the clerks who control so much of the destiny of the railway, or who did so at the time.

However, all was not gloom. I walked unaided for a further nine years and I was given the interesting task of going round all the BR Works to make a report. Transport and hotel expenses were provided. I had to report on the machinery and was often entertained by the Works Managers. After a spell at 222 Marylebone Road, I was sent to Derby Works, where the Works Manager was my old friend Peter Gray from Cowlairs days. He found me an office and I oversaw the progress on diesel shunters. But, after being used to a position of authority, I found it hard to accept that my career could no longer progress upward and, consequently, I took early retirement.

EPILOGUE

NOW that I am living in retirement, I can look back on a very interesting time on the railways and remember with gratitude Sir Nigel's influence. From my first sight of him at the Crimpsall, when he pushed the bucket of soapy water gently by the pit, I realised that he had the welfare of the men at heart. Shortly afterwards, proper washing facilities were provided. When I was a probationer draughtsman, I recall a letter from HNG proposing the provision of upholstered seats for all the Pacifics. Another letter came requesting sidescreens to protect the driver's eyes when sighting signals.

In any discussions of a technical nature, I was addressed as an equal. He was courteous and willing to listen to others and was convinced of the importance of the railways. Having recently read the marvellous books by Sir Winston Churchill, I realise how party political government has caused so many difficulties in the British Isles. The books reminded me of the truth of Sir Nigel's saying that railways are a national necessity.

The railway network is more durable than the road system, which is expensive in land use and to repair. Railways are a national resource which should be maximised by carrying freight and passengers to reduce road traffic, not least so that valuable land can be left undisturbed. The reduction of vibration damage resulting from a return to rail would benefit our city buildings too.

It is pleasing to reflect that the 'Gresley look' in a locomotive still produces the same happy reaction in anyone who has an eye for symmetry and beauty of line. We first felt this excitement at Doncaster when the conventional square front cab gave way to the V-front cab and the 'A4' began to take shape under our eyes. It is entirely fitting that his crowning achievement, 'A4' Pacific No 4498 *Sir Nigel Gresley*, should be preserved in good running order as a permanent reminder of a man of vision.